SAVED WITHOUT A DOUBT

JOHN MacARTHUR, JR.

While this book is intended for the reader's personal enjoyment and profit, it is also designed for group study. A personal and group study guide is located at the end of this text.

VICTOR BOOKS

A DIVISION OF SCRIPTURE PRESS PUBLICATIONS INC.
USA CANADA ENGLAND

A C K N O W L E D G M E N T S

Thanks to the staff of
Grace to You
who lent their editorial expertise to this project.
Particular thanks to Allacin Morimizu,
who arranged and edited this book
from sermon transcripts.

Unless otherwise noted, all Scripture references are from the *New American Standard Bible,* © the Lockman Foundation 1960, 1962, 1963, 1968, 1971, 1972, 1973, 1975, 1977. Other quotations are from the *Holy Bible, New International Version®* (NIV). Copyright © 1973, 1978, 1984 by International Bible Society. Used by permission of Zondervan Publishing House. All rights reserved; the *Authorized (King James) Version* (KJV); J.B. Phillips: *The New Testament in Modern English,* Revised Edition (PH), © J.B. Phillips, 1958, 1960, 1972, permission of Macmillan Publishing Co. and Collins Publishers; and *The New King James Version* (NKJV). © 1979, 1980, 1982, Thomas Nelson, Inc., Publishers.

Copyeditors: Jerry Yamamoto, Barbara Williams
Cover Design: Joe DeLeon
Cover Illustration: Joe DeLeon

Library of Congress Cataloging-in-Publication Data

MacArthur, John. 1939-
  Saved without a doubt / by John MacArthur, Jr.
    p.   cm.   — (The MacArthur study series)
  Includes indexes.
  ISBN 1-56476-017-0
  1. Assurance (Theology) I. Title. II. Series: MacArthur, John.
1939-   MacArthur study series.
BT785.M33   1992
234–dc20   92-27483
                                                          CIP

  3   4   5   6   7   8   9   10 Printing/Year 96   95   94   93

SAVED WITHOUT A DOUBT

C O N T E N T S

INTRODUCTION

It's a heartache to me as a pastor to realize that so many Christians lack assurance of their salvation. They lack the confidence that their sins are truly forgiven and their place in heaven is eternally secure. The pain I feel over this issue was heightened as I read this letter:

> I've been attending Grace Church for several years. As a result of a growing conviction in my heart, your preaching, and my seeming powerlessness against the temptations which arise in my heart and which I constantly succumb to, my growing doubts have led me to believe that I'm not saved.
>
> How sad it is, John, for me not to be able to enter in because of the sin which clings to me and from which I long to be free. How bizarre for one who has had advanced biblical training and who teaches in Sunday School with heartfelt conviction! So many times I have determined in my heart to repent, to shake loose my desire to sin, to forsake all for Jesus, only to find myself doing the sin I don't want to do and not doing the good I want to do.
>
> After my fiancée and I broke up, I memorized Ephesians as part of an all-out effort against sin, only to find myself weaker and more painfully aware of my sinfulness, more prone to sin than ever before, and grabbing cheap thrills to push back the pain of lost love. This occurs mostly in the heart, John, but that's where it counts and that's where we live. I sin because I'm a sinner. I'm like a soldier without armor running across a battlefield getting shot up by fiery darts from the enemy.
>
> I couldn't leave the church if I wanted to. I love the people, and I'm enthralled by the Gospel of the beautiful Messiah. But I'm a pile of manure on the white marble floor of Christ, a mongrel dog that sneaked in the back

door of the King's banquet to lick the crumbs off the floor, and by being close to Christians who are rich in the blessings of Christ, I get some of the overflow and ask you to pray for me as you think best.

I was struck by how eloquently the author of that poignant letter expressed his feelings—feelings I've discovered to be common among many sincere Christians. Yes, many.

Two years ago, as I began preaching through 2 Peter, I embarked on an eight-part study of the assurance of salvation. Invariably after each service, people would come to me and say, "Until tonight I have never experienced assurance." They repeatedly thanked me for speaking on the topic—and thanked God for the clarity of His Word on assurance.

That experience made me acutely aware of the need for biblical clarity on assurance—especially on how it relates to our emotions as believers. I found myself wondering how a person could take the monumental, life-changing step of becoming a Christian, yet not be assured of the results. My assurance is essential to the way I respond to life as a Christian. I cannot imagine living without it. Every true Christian should enjoy the reality of his or her salvation. Not to have that assurance is to live in doubt, fear, and a unique form of misery and spiritual depression.

Undeserved Assurance

Now some people have assurance who have no right to it. An old spiritual put it simply and directly: "Everybody talkin' about heaven ain't going there." Some feel all is well between them and God when it isn't. They don't understand the truth about salvation and their own spiritual condition.

Many people ask me why I speak and write so frequently on salvation and spiritual self-examination. Often they fear that what I've said will undermine the assurance of true Christians. Of course, I have no desire to do that, but to maintain a balanced perspective on the issue, I recall that Jesus said, "Not everyone who says to Me, 'Lord, Lord,' will enter the kingdom of heaven; but he who does the will of My Father, who is in heaven. Many will say to Me on that day, 'Lord, Lord, did we not prophesy in Your name, and in Your name cast out demons, and in Your name perform many miracles?' And then I will declare to them, 'I never knew you' " (Matt. 7:21-23). That passage haunts me. Like no other, it brings me face-to-face with the reality that *many* people are deceived about their salvation. I'm sure the Apostle Paul felt that way when he said to the church at large, "Test yourselves to see if you are in the faith; examine yourselves!" (2 Cor. 13:5)

How do people acquire a false sense of assurance? By receiving false information about salvation. Much of our modern-day evangelism contributes to that through what I call "syllogistic assurance."

A syllogism has a major premise and a minor premise that lead to a conclusion. Let's consider John 1:12: "As many as received Him, to them He gave the right to become children of God, even to those who believe in His name." The major premise: Anyone who receives Jesus becomes God's child. The minor premise: The person you just witnessed to received Christ. Conclusion: The person must now be a child of God. That seems logical, but the problem is, you don't know whether the minor premise is true—whether the person truly received Christ. Beware of trying to assure people of their salvation based on an untested profession. True assurance is the reward of tested and proven faith (James 1:2-4; 1 Peter 1:6-9). And it's the Holy Spirit who gives real assurance (Rom. 8:16). The human counselor must guard against any tendency to usurp that role.

Undermined Assurance

Some people believe no one can have real assurance—not even a true Christian. They reject God's sovereignty in salvation,

thereby destroying the theological basis for eternal security and
assurance. That's the historical Arminian view (named after a
Dutch theologian). It asserts that if a Christian thinks he is
secure forever, he is apt to become spiritually negligent.

That belief is also the official teaching of the Roman Catholic
Church. The Council of Trent declared it anathema to say "that
a man who is born again and justified is bound [of faith] to
believe that he is certainly in the number of the predestined"
(canon 15 on justification). Modern Catholic teaching, such as
that of Vatican II, upholds that position.

G.C. Berkhouwer's *The Conflict with Rome* explains that Rome's
denial of the assurance of salvation is consistent with its concep-
tion of the nature of salvation ([Philadelphia: Presbyterian and
Reformed, 1957], pp. 118–19). Since it conceives of salvation as a
joint effort by man and God, something that's maintained through
the doing of good works, it concludes the believer can never be
absolutely sure of his salvation. Why? Because if my salvation
depends on God *and* me, I might mess up.

Whenever you have a theology that involves human effort for
salvation, there can be no true security or assurance because
human beings can default. But historical biblical theology declares that salvation is entirely the work of God, which leads to
the concomitant doctrines of security and assurance.

The Apostle John said, "These things I have written to you
who believe in the name of the Son of God, in order that you
may *know* that you have eternal life" (1 John 5:13, emphasis
added). The Prophet Isaiah wrote, "The work of righteousness
will be peace, and the service of righteousness, quietness and
confidence forever" (Isa. 32:17). Where God grants righteousness, He also adds the peace of assurance.

Full Assurance
It's true that someone can be saved and doubt it. One may go to
heaven in a mist, not knowing for sure he's going, but that's
certainly not the way to enjoy the trip.

God wants you to enjoy that trip. First, consider what the Bible teaches about the lasting nature of salvation. There's no valid basis for being assured of your salvation if Scripture says it's possible for you to lose it. We will examine the classic biblical texts affirming the forever quality of salvation, but will not ignore the troubling passages that seem to indicate otherwise. Then we will explore two passages that overwhelmingly illustrate in cumulative fashion the security of salvation as a gift of God in line with His irrevocable purposes. All this constitutes the *objective grounds for assurance.* We're to be assured of our salvation first and foremost because Scripture *promises* eternal life to those who believe in Christ (John 20:31). God's Word and the guarantee of life to believers is thus the foundation of all assurance.

Second, once we've established that the Bible consistently affirms that salvation is forever, we need to get personal. As Paul said, we need to test ourselves. The lasting nature of salvation won't mean anything to you personally unless you are a genuine believer. How can you tell whether you really are a Christian? How do you know if your faith is real? The Apostle John wrote his first letter to answer that question, for it is the same question. He gave us a series of tests to measure ourselves by, and we will take them all. They delve into the *subjective grounds for assurance.* Their focus is the fruit of righteousness in the believer's life and the internal witness of the Holy Spirit. Note that those two subjective factors have meaning *only* if they are first rooted by faith in the objective truth of God's Word. They are vital to our discussion, however, and I will emphasize them in the remainder of the book because most contemporary discussions on assurance focus almost exclusively on the objective grounds for assurance. They minimize or dismiss the subjective grounds, thus robbing an untold number of believers of a valuable source of assurance. Worse yet, in doing so they perpetuate the tragic phenomenon of false assurance.

Third, as we take a closer look at the subjective grounds for

assurance, we will see what God's Word says to the many believers who struggle emotionally with the issue of assurance—in
spite of knowing the promises of Scripture. Perhaps you're one
of them: You believe in the security of salvation and that your
faith in Christ is genuine, but you are plagued with the insecure
feeling of not knowing for sure whether you will go to heaven.
For some of you, those times are but fleeting moments; for
others, they last a long time; and for still others, they seem like
a way of life. Is there any way to overcome that doubt? How can
you match up your feelings with your faith? How can you experience the assurance of your salvation?

For a start, it helps to know the different reasons that could
lead you to doubt your salvation. That's how I began my series
on assurance from 2 Peter 1. It's an honest examination of
where most of us are struggling. We don't want to assume that
because we know the facts, we therefore experience the reality.
That assurance will become more and more real as we understand and apply the virtues Peter described. After we examine
them in detail, we will conclude our study by taking an encouraging look at victory in the Spirit and the promise of God to
help us persevere.

To provide hooks to hang your thoughts on, I've come up
with three simple questions to remind you of the direction of
our study:

• *Is it a done deal?*—what the Bible teaches about the lasting
nature of salvation.

• *Is it real?*—how you can tell whether you are truly a
Christian.

• *Is it something I can feel?*—how you can experience the
assurance of a secure salvation.

My prayer is that after carefully considering each area, grace
and peace will be yours in fullest measure (1 Peter 1:2). Don't
continue to live with doubts about your eternal salvation. Rather, live with the blessed assurance God wants you to enjoy as
His child!

PART ONE:
IS IT A DONE DEAL?

What the Bible Teaches
about the Lasting
Nature of Salvation

ONE

A Collective Work

A rm locked in arm, deep in concentration, united in purpose, and falling to earth at almost 100 miles per hour, formation sky divers experience the exhilarating rewards not of luck but of hard work, preparation, and teamwork. The inherent dangers of formation skydiving require that each member work in harmony with the other members. Each individual must look out for the good of the group and not merely his or her own well-being. That kind of commitment enables the team to achieve graceful, awe-inspiring unity.

There's no greater illustration of such teamwork in the spiritual realm than the work of the Holy Trinity in securing our salvation. I believe Scripture makes that abundantly clear. In it we see no less than a collective work of the Father, Son, and Holy Spirit on our behalf.

The Sovereign Decree of the Father
Jesus said, "Truly, truly, I say to you, he who hears My word, and believes Him who sent Me, has eternal life, and does not come into judgment, but has passed out of death into life" (John 5:24). That may be the most monumental statement ever made in the Bible relative to the security of salvation. The believer

has received everlasting life and will not come under judgment.

Jesus also explained why the Father had sent the Son: "For God so loved the world, that He gave His only begotten Son, that whoever believes in Him should not perish, but have eternal life. . . . He who believes in Him is not judged; he who does not believe has been judged already" (John 3:16, 18). In a positive way Jesus tells us we have everlasting life. In a negative way He tells us we will never come into judgment.

In addition Jesus said, "All that the Father gives Me shall come to Me" (John 6:37). All whom God sovereignly chooses will come to Christ. However, what the Bible teaches regarding divine election should not restrain anyone from coming to Christ, for our Lord went on to say, "The one who comes to Me I will certainly not cast out" (v. 37).

Then Jesus said, "I have come down from heaven, not to do My own will, but the will of Him who sent Me. And this is the will of Him who sent Me, that of all that He has given Me I lose nothing, but raise it up on the last day" (vv. 38-39). All who are chosen for salvation—all who come to Jesus Christ—will be raised up at the great resurrection preceding His return to earth. Not one will be lost.

In verse 40, Jesus' teaching on the divine plan of salvation is summed up in this way: "This is the will of My Father, that every one who beholds the Son, and believes in Him, may have eternal life; and I Myself will raise him up on the last day." Whoever believes in Christ will be raised up to the fullness of eternal life. That is the will of the Father and the promise of God's Word.

Further on in John's Gospel, Jesus said, "My sheep hear My voice, and I know them, and they follow Me; and I give eternal life to them; and they shall never perish, and no one shall snatch them out of My hand. My Father, who has given them to Me, is greater than all; and no one is able to snatch them out of the Father's hand" (John 10:27-29). Picture the believer resting securely in Christ's hands, which in turn are clasped tightly by the Father's hands. Now that's a secure position! Yet some suggest that while God holds tightly onto us, perhaps we can leap or fall out of that heavenly grasp. Not so. God made an oath toward that end.

In Hebrews 6:13, 16-18, we read that since God "could swear by no one greater, He swore by Himself. . . . For men swear by one greater than themselves, and with them an oath given as confirmation is an end of every dispute. In the same way God, desiring even more to show to the heirs of the promise the unchangeableness of His purpose, interposed with an oath, in order that . . . we may have strong encouragement, we who have fled for refuge in laying hold of the hope set before us."

It was common in New Testament times for a person to make an oath on something or someone greater than himself. A Jewish man would swear by the altar of the temple, the high priest, or even God Himself. Once such an oath was made, the argument was over. It was assumed that if someone was willing to make such a serious oath, he was fully determined to keep it.

God, of course, doesn't need to make such an oath. His word is every bit as good without an oath—as ours ought to be (cf. Matt. 5:33-37). But to accommodate the weak faith of mere men and women, God made an oath of His promise to provide His children with a future hope. Since there is nothing or no one greater than God, He swore by Himself (Heb. 6:13). That pledge did not make God's promise any more secure; the bare Word of God is guarantee enough, but God gave an oath out of His kind consideration of us to affirm that He meant what He said.

His intent was to provide us with "strong encouragement" (v. 18). The Greek phrase so translated refers to a great source of consolation and confidence. "We who have fled for refuge" alludes to the Old Testament cities God had provided for people who sought protection from avengers for an accidental killing (cf. Num. 35; Deut. 19; Josh. 20). The Greek word translated "refuge" is the same one used in the Septuagint (the Greek version of the Old Testament) in those passages. We will never know whether God can hold onto us until we run in desperation to Him for refuge.

In what practical way can we run to Him? By "laying hold of the hope set before us" (v. 18). What is that hope? Christ Himself (1 Tim. 1:1) and the Gospel He brought (Col. 1:5). If you are ever going to have a strong confidence and a steadfast hope, you must seek refuge in God and embrace Jesus Christ, who is your only hope of salvation.

The High-Priestly Work of Christ

Hebrews 6:19-20 concludes with a description of our hope in Christ: "This hope we have as an anchor of the soul, a hope both sure and steadfast and one which enters within the veil, where Jesus has entered as a forerunner for us, having become a high priest forever according to the order of Melchizedek."

As our High Priest, Jesus serves as the anchor of our souls, who forever keeps us from drifting away from God. As a believer, your relationship with Christ anchors you to God. You can be confident because it is "within the veil" (v. 19). The most sacred place in the Jewish temple was the holy of holies, which was veiled from the rest of the temple. Inside the holy of holies rested the ark of the covenant, which signified the glory of God. Only once a year, on the Day of Atonement, could the high priest of Israel enter beyond the veil and make atonement for the sins of his people. But under the New Covenant, Christ made atonement once for all time and for all people by His sacrifice on the cross. The believer's soul is, in God's mind, already secured within the veil—His eternal sanctuary.

Once Jesus entered the heavenly holy of holies, He did not leave, as did the Jewish high priests. Rather, "He sat down at the right hand of the Majesty on high" (1:3). And Jesus remains there forever as the Guardian of our souls. Such absolute security is almost incomprehensible. Not only are our souls anchored within the impregnable, inviolable heavenly sanctuary, but our Savior, the Lord Jesus Christ, stands guard over them as well!

How can the Christian's security be described as anything but eternal? Truly we can entrust our souls with God and the Savior He provided.

While Jesus was on earth anticipating His high-priestly work to come, He prayed for His disciples, saying, "I am no more in the world; and yet they themselves are in the world, and I come to Thee. Holy Father, keep them in Thy name" (John 17:11). Jesus extended that prayer of protection beyond His apostles to us, who would come to believe in Christ through the apostles' teaching (v. 20). Since our Savior always prays in perfect harmony with the will of the Father, we can be assured that keeping our salvation secure is the will of God.

We are secured by the sovereign purpose of God and the continual, faithful intercession of our Great High Priest—the Lord Jesus Christ. Most appropriately does Jude praise Him who is able to keep us from stumbling, and to make us stand in the presence of His glory blameless with great joy (Jude 24).

The Seal of the Spirit

God's simple word about our security should be sufficient for us, but in His graciousness He makes His promises even more certain—if that were possible—by giving us His own special set of guarantees. In Ephesians 1:13-14, Paul tells us we were sealed in Christ "with the Holy Spirit of promise, who is given as a pledge of our inheritance, with a view to the redemption of God's own possession." The Lord is guaranteeing His promises with His seal and with His pledge. That is reminiscent of the passage we just examined in Hebrews 6, in which God gave His promise of blessing and then confirmed it with an oath to all who hope in Christ.

Because we do not directly and immediately receive the fullness of all God's promises when we first believe—since it is "reserved in heaven" for us according to 1 Peter 1:4—we may sometimes be tempted to doubt our salvation and wonder about the ultimate blessings that are supposed to accompany it. The

work of salvation in our lives remains incomplete—we still await
the redemption of our bodies (Rom. 8:23), which will occur
when Christ returns for us. Because we have not yet received
full possession of our inheritance, we may question its reality or
at least its greatness.

As one means of guaranteeing His promises, God seals us
with the presence of the Third Person of the Trinity. We receive the indwelling Holy Spirit at the moment of salvation, "for
by one Spirit we were all baptized into one body"—the body or
church of Christ (1 Cor. 12:13). In fact, "if anyone does not
have the Spirit of Christ, he does not belong to Him" (Rom.
8:9). Incredibly, the body of every true Christian is actually "a
temple of the Holy Spirit" (1 Cor. 6:19).

When a person becomes a Christian, the Holy Spirit takes up
residence in his or her life. He remains within to empower us,
equip us for ministry, and function through the gifts He has
given us. The Holy Spirit is our Helper and Advocate. He
protects and encourages us. He also assures us of our inheritance in Jesus Christ: "The Spirit Himself bears witness with our
spirit that we are children of God, and if children, heirs also,
heirs of God and fellow heirs with Christ" (Rom. 8:16-17). The
Spirit of God is our security, our special guarantee from God.

He has been given to us "as a pledge [Gk., arrabōn] of our
inheritance" (Eph. 1:14). Arrabōn originally referred to a down
payment or earnest money given to secure a purchase. Later it
came to represent any sort of pledge. A form of the word even
came to be used for an engagement ring.

As believers, we have the Holy Spirit as the divine pledge of
our inheritance, God's first installment of His guarantee that the
fullness of His promises will one day be completely fulfilled. We
are assured with an absolute certainty only God can provide.
The Holy Spirit is the church's irrevocable pledge, her divine
engagement ring signifying that as Christ's bride, she will never
be neglected or forsaken.

The Father's sovereign decree, the Son's intercessory ministry, and the Spirit's seal—they all work together magnificently in providing a secure salvation. Augustine well concluded that being assured of our salvation is no arrogant stoutness. It is faith. It is not presumption. Rather it is confidence in God's promise.

TWO

Those Troubling Verses

N o Christian can deny that the promises in Ephesians, John, and Hebrews regarding our secure salvation at the hands of our Triune God are indeed encouraging. Perhaps, however, you have been troubled by other sections of Scripture that seem to undermine those promises. What about Paul's statement to the Galatian church that some had fallen from grace? What about a less encouraging passage in Hebrews that speaks of those once enlightened who cannot be renewed to repentance? What about Jesus' frightening statement in John 15 that those who don't abide in Him are thrown away as dead branches, gathered up, and burned? What about perhaps His most frightening statement of all, in Matthew 12, where Jesus says there's such a thing as an unpardonable sin? Let's examine each passage in its context to determine what it's actually saying, and how each relates to the security of our salvation.

Galatians 5 and Falling from Grace
Our text begins:

It was for freedom that Christ set us free; therefore keep standing firm and do not be subject again to a yoke of

slavery. Behold I, Paul, say to you that if you receive circumcision, Christ will be of no benefit to you. And I testify
again to every man who receives circumcision, that he is
under obligation to keep the whole Law. You have been
severed from Christ, you who are seeking to be justified by
law; *you have fallen from grace*. For we through the Spirit,
by faith, are waiting for the hope of righteousness (vv. 1-5,
emphasis added).

Who is being addressed, and in what sense had they fallen
from grace?

All the people to whom Paul was writing had made a profession of Jesus Christ as Savior and Lord, or they would not have
been part of the churches of Galatia. Many had come from a
Jewish background emphasizing legalistic self-effort to please
God. Some were unable to set aside that background, even
though at first they responded positively to the Gospel message
of justification before God through faith in Christ alone.

Some of those individuals, known as Judaizers, created problems within churches by claiming that faith in Jesus Christ,
although important, was not sufficient for complete salvation.
They taught that what Moses began in the Old Covenant and
Christ added in the New Covenant had to be finished and
perfected by one's own efforts (circumcision being the center-
piece as a symbol of spiritual merit).

Paul combated that heretical notion by pointing out four of
its tragic consequences. In Galatians 5, he declares that regardless of someone's association with the church, if he by his life or
words rejects the sufficiency of faith in Christ, he forfeits
Christ's work on his behalf, places himself under obligation to
keep the whole Mosaic Law, falls from God's grace, and ex-
cludes himself from God's righteousness.

We as Christians believe salvation is by grace through faith.
The Judaizers at first seemed to acknowledge that concept, but
then fell away from it by emphasizing the Mosaic Law as the

means to salvation. That's what it means to have fallen from grace. To attempt to be justified by Law is to reject the way of grace.

In Galatians 5:4, Paul was not referring to the security of the believer but to the contrasting ways of grace and law, faith and works, as means of salvation. He certainly wasn't teaching that a person who has once been justified can lose his righteous standing before God and become lost again by being legalistic. The Bible knows nothing of becoming *unjustified.*

Applied to one who was really an unbeliever, the principle of falling from grace speaks of being exposed to the gracious truth of the Gospel and then turning one's back on Christ. Such a person is an apostate.

During the time of the early church, many unbelievers—both Jews and Gentiles—not only heard the Gospel but also witnessed the miraculous confirming signs performed by the apostles. They often couldn't help becoming attracted to Christ and making some profession of faith in Him. Many became involved in a local church and vicariously experienced the blessings of Christian love and fellowship. They were exposed firsthand to every truth and blessing of the Gospel of grace, but then turned away. According to a passage we will soon examine, they had "been enlightened," had "tasted of the heavenly gift," and had even "been made partakers of the Holy Spirit" by witnessing His divine ministry in the lives of believers (Heb. 6:4). But they refused to trust in Christ alone, so they fell away, losing all prospect of repentance and therefore of salvation, since "there is salvation in no one else; for there is no other name under heaven . . . by which we must be saved" (Acts 4:12). They came to the very doorway of grace and then fell away, back into their works-oriented religion.

Hebrews 6 and Those Once Enlightened

It is possible for people to go to church for years, hear the Gospel over and over again, and even be faithful church members, but never commit their lives to Jesus Christ. We meet such people in Hebrews 6. The writer was specifically talking to Jewish people similar to the legalistic Galatians, but the warning applies to anyone.

Many sincere Christians take that warning too far, however, as Hannah Hurnard movingly illustrated in one of her allegories. Mercy consoles her heartbroken friend Umbrage and begins speaking to her about the Lord:

> "Umbrage, you are forgetting. There is a solution, quite a different one, to your problem. You know what the solution is. You must tell the Shepherd what you have told me and ask him what you are to do. And then, 'Whatsoever he saith unto you, do it.' "
>
> "The Shepherd!" wailed Umbrage in a desolate voice. "The Shepherd will never speak to me again. I have turned my back upon him and have disobeyed his voice. He will not help me now, Mercy, for he warned me what would happen. And I hardened my heart and would not listen, and I 'have done despite to the Spirit of Grace,' and have 'drawn back,' and he will say that it is impossible to do anything for me for I have brought everything upon myself by disobedience. Oh, if only I had listened to him! If only I could go back to the time before I sinned!"
>
> "He will say nothing of the sort," cried Mercy earnestly. "You know, you must know, that you are saying what is not true about him. Why, he has only waited with the utmost love and patience until the time should come when you would be ready at last to listen to him and to seek his help."
>
> "Then what is the meaning of that terrible passage in the Scriptures?" asked Umbrage despairingly, "which says: 'Of how much sorer punishment . . . shall he be thought worthy, who hath trodden under foot the Son of God . . . and hath done despite unto the Spirit of Grace . . .' 'If we

sin willfully after that we have received the knowledge of
the truth, there remaineth no more sacrifice for sins,
but a certain fearful looking for of judgment and fiery
indignation.' 'It is impossible for those who were once enlightened, and have tasted of the heavenly gift . . . If they
shall fall away, to renew them again unto repentance; seeing they crucify to themselves the Son of God afresh, and
put him to an open shame' " (Heb. 10:29, 26, 27; 6:4-6).

"Dear Umbrage," said Mercy earnestly, "do you not see
that those verses do not and cannot apply to you, for you
are repentant? You do not need me or anyone else to try to
persuade or force you to repent. The sure evidence that
one had done despite to the Spirit of Grace is that he has
lost all power to desire repentance and restoration. Indeed,
he wants to go on crucifying the Son of God afresh and to
reject the Holy Spirit. But you! You are longing beyond all
words to be restored and to be in communion with the
Savior again, and you can find no rest or peace until you
are. That is a sure sign that his Spirit is even now working
in you and beginning to restore you."

"But," said Umbrage, still in a tone of utter despair, "what
about that verse which says that Esau, when he wanted to
repent, could not do so? 'Ye know how that afterward, when
he would have inherited the blessing he was rejected: for he
found no place of repentance, though he sought it carefully
with tears' (Heb. 12:17). You see, it was too late for him to
be forgiven even when he wanted to repent."

"It doesn't say anything of the sort," answered Mercy
cheerfully and firmly. "You have got it all wrong, Umbrage! It
does say that Esau sold his birthright for one morsel of meat,
and then afterwards, when he was sorry that he had done so
and would have liked to inherit the firstborn son's blessing
after all, it belonged to Jacob. And though he repented with
tears that he had despised the birthright blessing of the elder
son, it was too late for him to get it back.

"But that is quite a different thing from saying that though you are now sorry you disobeyed the Shepherd he will not forgive you. Do you not see, dear Umbrage, the real meaning of the verse? Like Esau you did despise the Shepherd's offer to take you to the High Places because you did prefer and choose to marry Resentment. And that you cannot alter. What is done cannot be undone even though I find you weeping your heart out here in the garden and repenting of the wrong choice which you made in bitterness and despair. You are married to Resentment, and you are the daughter-in-law of poor old Mrs. Sullen, and there is no getting away from the fact, however much you now regret it. In that sense what is done cannot be undone in spite of your repentance. But that is not to say that the Shepherd no longer loves and owns you, or that he will refuse to help you. It means that you need him more than ever before in these terribly difficult and tragic circumstances into which you have got yourself.

"Oh, my dear, dear Umbrage, will you not realize this at last and lose not a moment longer in seeking his help? For you know quite well that he can change everything completely and bring victory out of defeat, which is the thing he loves to do most of all." (From *Mountains of Spices*, pp. 155–159, by Hannah Hurnard, © 1977 Tyndale House Publishers, Inc. Used by permission. All rights reserved.)

It is encouraging to know what God can do with a repentant heart. But it should make the hairs on your neck stand up on end knowing what He will do with unrepentant sinners. In particular, those who know the truth of God's saving grace in Jesus Christ—who perhaps have seen it change the lives of many of their friends and family members, who may even have made some profession of faith in Him—yet who turn around and walk away from full acceptance, are given the severest possible warning. Persistent rejection of Christ will result in such persons' passing the point of no return spiritually, of losing forever the opportunity of salvation. That is what always happens to the individual who is indecisive. He eventually follows his evil heart of unbelief and turns his back forever on the living God.

Unlike a knife, truth becomes sharper with use, which for truth comes by acceptance and obedience. A truth that is heard but not accepted and followed becomes dull and meaningless. The more we neglect it, the more immune to it we become. By not accepting the Gospel when it was still "news," those addressed in the Book of Hebrews had begun to grow indifferent to it and had become spiritually sluggish, neglectful, and hard. Because of the disuse of their knowledge of the Gospel, they now could not bring themselves to make the right decision about it. They were, in fact, in danger of making a desperately wrong decision, of turning around because of pressure and persecution, and completely going back to Judaism.

The individuals addressed here had five great advantages because of their association with the church: They had been enlightened, had tasted Christ's heavenly gift, had partaken of the Holy Spirit, had tasted the Word of God, and had tasted the miraculous powers of the age to come (vv. 4-5). There is no reference at all to salvation. In fact, no term used here is ever used elsewhere in the New Testament for salvation, and none should be taken to refer to it in this passage.

The enlightenment spoken of here has to do with intellectual perception of spiritual truth. It means to be mentally aware of something, to be instructed, informed. It carries no connotation of response—of acceptance or rejection, belief or disbelief. The tasting or partaking implies something similar: a mere sampling of truth. It was not embraced or lived, only examined.

These individuals had been wondrously blessed by God's enlightenment, by association with His Spirit, and by sampling His heavenly gifts, His Word, and His power. Still they did not believe. Hence comes the fearful warning that for those who have experienced all that, "and then have fallen away, it is impossible to renew them again to repentance, since they again crucify to themselves the Son of God, and put Him to open shame" (Heb. 6:6).

Because they believe that warning is addressed to Christians, some interpreters think Hebrews 6 teaches that salvation can be lost. If that interpretation were true, however, the passage would also teach that, once lost, salvation could never be regained— that the person would be damned forever. There would be no going back and forth, in and out of grace, as most people who believe you can lose your salvation seem to assume. But Christians are not being addressed, and it is the opportunity for receiving salvation, not salvation itself, that can be lost.

It is unbelievers who are in danger of losing salvation—in the sense of losing the opportunity ever to receive it. Once they see and hear the truth of the Gospel, they have only two choices: either going on to full knowledge of God through faith in Christ or turning away from Him and becoming lost forever. The frightening finality of that danger must not be minimized.

A vaccination immunizes by giving a very mild case of the disease. People who are exposed to the Gospel can get just enough of it to immunize them against the real thing. The longer they continue to resist it, whether graciously or violently, the more they become immune to it. Their spiritual system becomes more and more unresponsive and insensitive. Their only hope is to reject whatever they are holding onto and re-ceive Christ without delay—lest they become so hard, often without knowing it, that their opportunity is forever lost. When people reject Christ at the peak experience of knowledge and conviction, they will not accept Him at a lesser level. So salva-tion becomes impossible.

Our passage in Hebrews closes with a vivid illustration: "Ground that drinks the rain which often falls upon it and brings forth vegetation useful to those for whose sake it is also tilled, receives a blessing from God; but if it yields thorns and thistles, it is worthless and close to being cursed, and it ends up being burned" (vv. 7-8). All who hear the Gospel are like the earth. Just like the rain, the Gospel message falls on its hearers. After the Gospel seed is planted, there is nourishment and growth. Some of the growth is good and productive, but some of it is false, spurious, and unproductive. While all growth comes from the same seed and is nourished by the same ground and the same water, some of it becomes thorny, destructive, and worthless. It rejects the life offered and is fit only for burning.

John 15 and the Burning Branches
Burning useless growth is an evocative analogy used frequently in Scripture to describe apostasy. We find it and others like it in many of Jesus' parables (e.g., Matt. 13:24-30, 36-43; 18:23-35; 22:1-14; Luke 3:7-9). Our Lord's use of it in John 15 has troubled many believers:

> I am the true vine, and My Father is the vinedresser. Every branch in Me that does not bear fruit, He takes away; and every branch that bears fruit, He prunes it, that it may bear more fruit. . . . Abide in Me, and I in you. As the branch cannot bear fruit of itself, unless it abides in the vine, so neither can you, unless you abide in Me. . . . If anyone does not abide in Me, he is thrown away as a branch, and dries up; and they gather them, and cast them into the fire, and they are burned (vv. 1-2, 4, 6).

In first-century Palestine, it was common to prevent a vine from bearing fruit for three years after it was first planted. In the fourth year it was strong enough to bear fruit. Its fruit-bearing capacity had been increased by careful pruning. Mature branches, which had already been through the four-year process, were pruned annually from December through January so they would continue to be fruitful.

It is the essence of the Christian life to bear fruit. In Ephesians 2:10 Paul says, "We are His workmanship, created in

Christ Jesus for good works, which God prepared beforehand, that we should walk in them." The fruit of salvation is good works. In James 2:17, James explains that "faith, if it has no works, is dead, being by itself." If saving faith is present, it can't help but produce fruit. Good works don't save a person, but they do show that his or her faith is genuine.

In John 15, Jesus likened His followers to branches that bear fruit but need pruning now and then. There is no such thing as a fruitless Christian. Everyone bears some fruit. You may have to look hard to find even a small grape, but if you look close enough, you will find something.

Since all Christians bear fruit, it is clear that the fruitless branches in John 15 cannot refer to them. In fact, the fruitless branches had to be eliminated and thrown into the fire. Yet Jesus referred to the fruitless branches as those who were in Him (v. 2). Doesn't that imply they had to have been genuine believers?

Not necessarily. Externally they may be attached, but no life flows through them. Other passages in Scripture show it is possible to be a parasite on the vine, seemingly a part of it, but only in appearance. In Romans 9:6, for example, Paul says, "They are not all Israel who are descended from Israel." It was possible for a person to be part of the nation of Israel, yet not be a true Israelite. Likewise, it is possible to be a branch without abiding in the true vine. A similar metaphor in Romans represents Israel as an olive tree from which God had removed certain branches (11:17-24). Those branches were cut off because of unbelief.

Some only appear to be a part of God's people. In Luke 8:18, Jesus says, "Take care how you listen; for whoever has, to him shall more be given; and whoever does not have, even what he thinks he has shall be taken away from him." Appearance devoid of reality is grounds for being removed from God's people. One day the tares will be separated from the wheat on that basis (Matt. 13:30, 38).

Scripture issues a stern warning for us to check our own lives and make sure our salvation is genuine. The consequence is serious: A branch that does not bear fruit is taken away and burned.

For the believer, however, abiding in the true vine provides the deepest kind of security. "There is," Paul says, "no condemnation for those who are in Christ Jesus" (Rom. 8:1). Those who are in Him cannot be removed, they cannot be cut off, and they need not fear judgment. There is no suggestion here that those who now abide might later cease to do so.

On the other hand, those who do not abide will be judged. Jesus said, "If anyone does not abide in Me, he is thrown away as a branch, and dries up; and they gather them, and cast them into the fire, and they are burned" (John 15:6). Since they have no living connection to Jesus Christ, they are cast out.

The true believer, in contrast, can never be thrown away. As we noted previously in John 6:37, Jesus said, "All that the Father gives Me shall come to Me; and the one who comes to Me I will certainly not cast out." John later wrote, "They went out from us, but they were not really of us; for if they had been of us, they would have remained with us; but they went out, in order that it might be shown that they all are not of us" (1 John 2:19). If a person leaves the fellowship of God's people and never comes back, he or she was never a true believer to begin with.

William Pope was a member of the Methodist Church in England for most of his life. He made a pretense of knowing Christ and served in many capacities. Meanwhile, his wife died a genuine believer.

Soon, however, he began to drift from Christ. He had companions who believed in the redemption of demons. He began going with them to a house of prostitution. In time he became a drunkard.

He admired the skeptic Thomas Paine, and on Sundays he and his friends assembled to confirm one another in their infidelity. They amused themselves by throwing the Bible on the floor and kicking it around.

Eventually Pope contracted tuberculosis. Someone visited him and told him of the great Redeemer. He told Pope he could be saved from being punished for his sins.

But Pope replied, "I have no contrition; I cannot repent. God will damn me! I know the day of grace is lost. God has said to such as me, 'I will laugh at your calamity, and mock when your fear cometh.' I have denied Him; my heart is hardened."

Then he cried, "Oh, the hell, the pain I feel! I have chosen my way. I have done the horrible damnable deed: I have crucified the Son of God afresh; I have counted the blood of the covenant an unholy thing! Oh that wicked and horrible thing of blaspheming the Holy Spirit, which I know that I have committed; I want nothing but hell! Come, oh devil and take me!" (recounted in *Voices from the Edge of Eternity,* John Myers, ed. [Old Tappan, N.J.: Spire, 1972], pp. 147–49)

He spent most of his life in the church, but his end was infinitely worse than his beginning. Every man and woman has the same choice. You can abide in the vine and receive all of God's blessings, or you can be burned.

It doesn't seem like a difficult choice, does it? Yet millions of people resist God's gift of salvation, preferring the superficial relationship of the false branch.

We who abide in Christ are to let the warnings in Scripture motivate us to say to such people, "Behold, now is 'the acceptable time,' behold, now is 'the day of salvation' " (2 Cor. 6:2; Isa. 49:2). But don't let the salvation you proclaim be any less than it is: a glorious, secure salvation in total contrast to the unstable state of the unbeliever flirting on the fringes of faith.

Matthew 12 and the Unpardonable Sin

Let's take this a step further with an actual case study—a man who hears the call of salvation and responds. He starts reading Christian books. His mind, excitable by nature and undisciplined academically, begins to be fearfully disordered. He becomes preoccupied with religious externals, spending an inordinate amount of time in religious activities and feeling obliged to give up every innocent earthly enjoyment. He begins to look for miracles to confirm his faith.

Things become darker still: He's now convinced he's committed the unpardonable sin mentioned by Jesus. That leads him to envy the beasts of the field, the birds in the air, the stones on the street, and the tiles on the roof, for they are incapable of the blasphemy his conscience so searingly accuses him of. His emotional state destroys his power of digestion. His pain is such that he expects to burst asunder like Judas, whom he has come to regard as his prototype.

At length the clouds break. The man who thought he was destined to the same end as that of the arch-traitor comes to enjoy peace and assurance in the mercy of God. You can read his story in his autobiography, *Grace Abounding to the Chief of Sinners*. His name is John Bunyan, author of *The Pilgrim's Progress*, one of the most popular books of all time.

Bunyan isn't the only believer to fear committing the unpardonable sin. Many Christians have suffered that torment. Part of the reason is that some respected pastors and commentators imply that believers are capable of committing the sin Jesus so frighteningly spoke of, associating it with the "sin unto death" mentioned in 1 John 5:16 and the negligence of the enlightened ones we just examined in Hebrews 6:4-6.

I take great exception with that interpretation, for it disregards the context of Jesus' alarming statement. The passage is Matthew 12:22-31. Jesus heals a demon-possessed man, but when the religious leaders hear about it, they say, "This man casts out demons only by Beelzebub the ruler of the demons" (v. 24). Beelzebub, the lord of the flies, was a Philistine deity. He was believed to be the prince of evil spirits, and his name became another term for Satan. Those blind religious leaders were claiming that Jesus got His power from Satan.

Now Jesus' public ministry had been going on for over two years. During that time He had performed numerous miracles

that proved to all Israel He was God. But the religious establish-
ment essentially concluded the opposite.

Jesus received the power of the Holy Spirit at His baptism
(Matt. 3:16), at which time He began to prove who He really
was. At the same time Jesus always attributed His power to the
Spirit of God. As Isaiah predicted, the Spirit came upon Him
and He preached and did miracles (Isa. 61:1-2). Yet the religious leaders stated that His power was satanic.

Jesus gave a dry response to that claim: "If I'm casting out
Satan by using Satan's power, what do you think Satan is doing
to himself?" (Matt. 12:26, paraphrase) Obviously, the devil
would be destroying his own kingdom, which would make no
sense at all. The religious leaders' hatred and jealousy drove
them to such twisted logic. Instead of being rational, they were
being ridiculous.

Therefore Jesus said, "Any sin and blasphemy shall be forgiv-
en men, but blasphemy against the Spirit shall not be forgiven.
And whoever shall speak a word against the Son of Man, it shall
be forgiven him; but whoever shall speak against the Holy
Spirit, it shall not be forgiven him, either in this age, or in the
age to come" (vv. 31-32).

To conclude that Christ's miraculous works—affected by the
Holy Spirit to prove Christ's deity—were actually done by Satan
is to be in a hopeless state of rejection. Since the religious
leaders had seen and heard all that Jesus had done and said, yet
were still convinced it was satanic, they were obviously in a
hopeless state before God. They had concluded the opposite of
what was clearly true, and they had done so despite full
revelation.

What does that say to us? What is the application for today?
In the first place, this was a unique historical event that occurred when Christ was physically on earth. Since He isn't now,
there is no primary application. Perhaps there will be in "the age
to come" (the millennial kingdom), when Christ is again on the
earth.

Is there a secondary application? Yes, that unregenerate people can be forgiven anything if they are willing to repent and come to Christ. But continual, unrepentant blasphemy against the convincing and convicting work of the Holy Spirit, defined as fully knowing the facts about Jesus but nonetheless attributing His works to the devil, cannot be forgiven.

According to John 16, the Holy Spirit points to Jesus Christ, convicting the world of sin, righteousness, and judgment (vv. 7-11). Earlier John had written that everyone needs to be "born again" of the Spirit (3:1-8). Since it is the Holy Spirit who is the regenerative agent of the Trinity, anyone who is saved must eventually respond to His leading. If a person determines instead to reject and scorn the convicting work of the Spirit, there is no way that person can become a Christian.

During World War II, an American naval force in the North Atlantic was engaged in heavy battle with enemy ships and submarines on an exceptionally dark night. Six planes took off from a carrier to search out those targets, but while they were in the air, a total blackout was ordered for the carrier to protect it from attack. Without lights on the carrier's deck, the six planes could not possibly land. The pilots radioed a request for the lights to be turned on just long enough for them to come in. But because the entire carrier, with its several thousand men as well as all the other planes and equipment, would have been put in jeopardy, no lights were permitted to be turned on. When the six planes ran out of fuel, they crashed into the freezing water and all crew members perished into eternity.

There comes a time when the lights go out, when further opportunity for salvation is forever lost. One who rejects the full light can have no more light—and no forgiveness. May that strike terror into the hearts of all who now reject Christ, but not those who have embraced Him as Savior and Lord.

THREE

The Ties That Bind

A while ago my youngest daughter told me of a debate she had with a school friend. "Dad," she said, "what verse can you give me to prove salvation is secure?" Dozens came to mind! Some we have already surveyed, but the passage that most strongly impressed itself on my mind at the time is one you rarely hear mentioned in the debate over eternal security: Romans 5:1-11. That is a shame because it represents some of the Apostle Paul's most profound thinking on the topic.

To see that passage for what it is, we need to pay attention to how it fits into the Book of Romans. In the first three chapters, Paul proved that the whole world is guilty before God and that a person is made right with God only by "being justified as a gift by His grace through the redemption which is in Christ Jesus" (Rom. 3:24). That being the case, the question Paul anticipated his readers would have on their minds is: *Under what conditions then, is redemption preserved? By one's good works?*

Think about that. If the preservation of salvation depends on what believers themselves do or do not do, their salvation is only as secure as their faithfulness, which provides no security at all. According to that view, believers must protect by their own human power what Christ began by His divine power.

To counteract such presumption and its consequent hopeless-ness, Paul assured the Ephesian church with these comforting words: "I pray that the eyes of your heart may be enlightened, so that you may know what is the hope of His calling, what are the riches of the glory of His inheritance in the saints, and what is the surpassing greatness of His power toward us who believe. These are in accordance with the working of the strength of His might which He brought about in Christ, when He raised Him from the dead, and seated Him at His right hand in the heaven-ly places" (Eph. 1:18-20). Paul's prayer was that we as believers would be aware of the security we now and forever will have in Christ—a security that does not depend on our own feeble efforts, but on the "surpassing greatness of His power toward us." That truth is the basis for feeling assured.

Our hope is not in ourselves but in our great God, who is faithful. Isaiah described God's faithfulness as "the belt about His waist" (Isa. 11:5). David declared that the Lord's "faithful-ness reaches to the skies" (Ps. 36:5), and Jeremiah praised Him by exclaiming, "Great is Thy faithfulness" (Lam. 3:23). The writer of Hebrews said, "Let us hold fast the confession of our hope without wavering, for He who promised is faithful" (Heb. 10:23). While continued faith is necessary, our ability to hold fast is founded upon the Lord's faithfulness, not our own.

In developing his argument against the destructive notion that believers must live in uncertainty about the completion of their salvation, Paul presented six links in the chain of truth that binds all true believers eternally to their Savior and Lord: peace with God (Rom. 5:1), standing in grace (v. 2), hope of glory (vv. 2-5), possession of divine love (vv. 5-8), certainty of deliverance (vv. 9-10), and joy in the Lord (v. 11).

No More War

Paul begins Romans 5 by saying, "Therefore having been justi-fied by faith, we have peace with God through our Lord Jesus Christ." The first word connects Paul's present argument with what he had already said, especially in chapters 3 and 4, in which he established that, as believers, we have been justified by faith in Christ. Peace with God is one of the many great results.

The peace spoken of here is not subjective but objective. It is not a feeling but a fact. Apart from salvation through Jesus Christ, every human being is spiritually at war with God—regardless of what his or her feelings about God may be. In the same way, the person who is justified by faith in Christ is at peace with God, regardless of how he or she may feel about it at any given moment. Through trust in Jesus Christ, a sinner's war with God is ended for all eternity.

Most non-Christians don't think of themselves as enemies of God. Because they have no conscious feelings of hatred for Him and do not actively oppose His work or contradict His Word, they consider themselves—at worst—to be neutral about God. But no such neutrality is possible. The mind of every unsaved person is at peace only with the things of the flesh, and is therefore, by definition, "hostile toward God" (Rom. 8:7). It cannot be otherwise.

After missionary David Livingstone had spent several years among the Zulus of South Africa, he went with his wife and young child into the interior to minister. When he returned, he discovered that an enemy tribe had attacked the Zulus, killed many of the people, and taken the chief's son captive. The Zulu chief didn't want to make war with the other tribe, but he poignantly asked Dr. Livingstone, "How can I be at peace with them while they hold my son prisoner?"

Commenting on that story, Donald Grey Barnhouse wrote, "If this attitude is true in the heart of a savage chief, how much more is it true of God the Father toward those who trample under foot His Son, who count the blood of the covenant wherewith they were set apart as an unholy thing, and who continue to despise the Spirit of grace (Heb. 10:29)?" (*God's River: Romans 5:1-11* [Grand Rapids: Eerdmans, 1959], p. 26)

Not only are all unbelievers enemies of God, but God is also the enemy of all unbelievers—to the degree that He is angry with them every day (Ps. 7:11) and condemns them to eternal hell. God is the enemy of the sinner, and that enmity cannot end unless and until the sinner places his or her trust in Jesus Christ. To those who think God is too loving to send anyone to hell, Paul declared, "Let no one deceive you with empty words, for because of these things [the sins listed in Eph. 5:5] the wrath of God comes upon the sons of disobedience" (v. 6).

A professional football coach once said during a pregame devotional service I held for his team, "I don't know if there is a God, but I like having these chapels, because if there is one, I want to be sure He's on my side." Sentiments such as that are frequently expressed by unbelievers who think that the Creator and Sustainer of the universe can be cajoled into doing one's bidding by giving Him superficial lip service. God is never on the side of unbelievers. He is their enemy, and His wrath against them can be placated only by their trusting in the atoning work of His Son, Jesus Christ.

On the cross Christ took upon Himself all the fury of God's wrath that sinful humanity deserves. And those who trust in Christ are no longer God's enemies and under His wrath, but are at peace with Him.

The most immediate consequence of justification is reconciliation, which is the theme of Romans 5. Reconciliation with God brings peace with God. That peace is permanent and irrevocable because Jesus Christ, through whom believers receive their reconciliation, "always lives to make intercession for them" (Heb. 7:25). "For I will be merciful to their iniquities," the Lord says of those who belong to Him, "and I will remember their sins no more" (8:12; cf. 10:17). If anyone is ever to be punished in the future for the sins of believers, it would have to be the One who took them on Himself—Jesus Christ. But that is impossible, for He has already paid the penalty in full.

When a person embraces Jesus Christ in repentant faith, Christ Himself establishes eternal peace between that person and God the Father. In fact, Christ not only brings peace to the believer, but "He Himself is our peace" (Eph. 2:14), which points out how crucial it is to see the nature and extent of Christ's atoning work as the basis for our assurance.

Although the peace spoken of in Romans 5 is the objective peace of being reconciled to God, awareness of that objective truth gives the believer a deep and wonderful subjective peace as well. Knowing you are a child of God and a brother or sister of Jesus Christ cannot help but quiet your soul.

Knowing you are eternally at peace with God prepares you to wage effective spiritual warfare on Christ's behalf and in His power. When engaged in battle, a Roman soldier wore boots with spikes on the bottom to give him firm footing. Because you as a Christian have your feet shod with "the Gospel of peace" (Eph. 6:15), knowing God is on your side, you can have the confidence to stand firmly for Christ without the spiritual slipping and emotional sliding that uncertainty about salvation inevitably causes.

A Secure Standing

In Romans 5:2, Paul tells us that "through [Christ] also we have obtained our introduction by faith into this grace in which we stand." A second link in the unbreakable chain that eternally binds us to Christ is our standing in God's grace.

For the Jewish people, the idea of having direct access or "introduction" to God was unthinkable. To see God face-to-face was to die. After the tabernacle was built, and later the temple, strict boundaries were set. Gentiles could go only into the outer confines and no farther. Jewish women could go beyond the Gentile limit, but not much farther. And so it was with the men and the regular priests. Only the high priest could enter the holy of holies, where God would manifest His divine presence—but only once a year and very briefly. Even the high priest could lose his life if he entered unworthily. Bells were sewn onto the special garments he wore on the Day of Atonement, and if the sound of the bells stopped while he was ministering in the holy of holies, the people knew he had been struck dead by God (Ex. 28:35).

But Christ's death ended that. Through His atoning sacrifice, He made God the Father accessible to any person, Jew or Gentile, who trusts in that sacrifice. That's why the Book of Hebrews urges us to "draw near with confidence to the throne of grace, that we may receive mercy and may find grace to help in time of need" (Heb. 4:16).

To make that truth graphic, when Jesus was crucified, "the curtain of the temple was torn in two from top to bottom" by God's power (Matt. 27:51). His death forever removed the barrier to God's holy presence that the temple veil represented. The writer of Hebrews, commenting on that amazing truth, said, "Since therefore, brethren, we have confidence to enter the holy place by the blood of Jesus, by a new and living way which He inaugurated for us through the veil, that is, His flesh, and since we have a great priest over the house of God, let us draw near with a sincere heart in full assurance of faith, having our hearts sprinkled clean from an evil conscience, and our bodies washed with pure water" (Heb. 10:19-22).

On the basis of our faith in Him, Jesus Christ ushers us into this grace in which we stand. The Greek word translated "stand" in Romans 5:2 (histemi) carries the idea of permanence—of standing firm and immovable. Although faith is necessary for salvation, it is God's grace—not the believer's faith—that has the power to save and to keep him or her saved. We are not saved by divine grace and then preserved by human effort. That would be a mockery of God's grace, meaning that what God begins in us He is either unwilling or unable to preserve and complete. Paul unequivocally declared to the Philippian believers, "I am confident of this very thing, that He who began a good work in you will perfect it until the day of Christ Jesus" (Phil. 1:6). Emphasizing that same sublime truth, Jude spoke of Christ as "Him who is able to keep you from stumbling, and to make you stand in the presence of His glory blameless with great joy" (Jude 24). We do not begin in the Spirit to be perfected by the flesh (Gal. 3:3).

Believers will often fall into sin, but their sin is not more powerful than God's grace. They are the very sins for which Jesus paid the penalty. If no sin a person commits prior to his or her conversion is too great for Christ's atoning death to cover, surely no sin he or she commits afterward is too great to be covered. "For if while we were enemies," Paul reasoned, "we were reconciled to God through the death of His Son, much more, having been reconciled, we shall be saved by His life" (Rom. 5:10). If a dying Savior could bring us to God's grace, surely a living Savior can keep us in His grace.

To Timothy, his beloved son in the faith, Paul asserted with the utmost confidence: "I know whom I have believed and I am convinced that He is able to guard what I have entrusted to Him until that day" (2 Tim. 1:12). With equal certainty he wrote, "What then shall we say to these things? If God is for us, who is against us? He who did not spare His own Son, but delivered Him up for us all, how will He not also with Him freely give us all things? Who will bring a charge against God's elect? God is the One who justifies; who is the One who condemns? Christ Jesus is He who died, yes, rather who was raised, who is at the right hand of God, who also intercedes for us" (Rom. 8:31-34).

Since God sovereignly declares those of us who believe in His Son to be forever just, who can overturn that verdict? What higher court can overrule that divine acquittal?

Now it is not that believers may be free to sin that God has so soundly secured their salvation. The very purpose and effect of salvation is to free men and women from sin, not to free them to do it. Paul later reminded the Roman believers, "Having been freed from sin, you became slaves of righteousness" (Rom. 6:18). Yet Scripture repeatedly details the sinfulness, frailty, and weakness of men and women, including believers, and sensible and honest people can see those self-evident truths for themselves. Only self-delusion can lead Christians to believe that, in their own weakness and imperfection, they can preserve the great gift of spiritual life that could only be bought by the precious, sinless blood of God's own Son.

For believers to doubt their security is to question God's integrity and power. It is to add the merit of human works to the gracious, unmerited work of God. And it is to add self-trust to trust in our Lord, because if salvation can be lost by anything that we can or cannot do, our ultimate trust must obviously be in ourselves rather than in God.

Hope for the Future

A third link in the unbreakable chain that eternally binds us to Christ is this: "We exult in hope of the glory of God. And not only this, but we also exult in our tribulations; knowing that tribulation brings about perseverance; and perseverance, proven character; and proven character, hope; and hope does not disappoint" (Rom. 5:2-5).

Since every aspect of salvation is solely the work of God, it cannot possibly be lost. And the end of that marvelous work is the ultimate glorification of every believer in Jesus Christ, for those "whom [God] foreknew, He also predestined to become conformed to the image of His Son, that He might be the firstborn among many brethren; and whom He predestined, these He also called; and whom He called, these He also justified; and whom He justified, these He also glorified" (8:29-30).

As Paul has already established, salvation is *anchored in the past* because Christ has made peace with God for all those who trust in Him. It is *anchored in the present* because, by Christ's continual intercession, every believer now stands securely in God's grace. Now Paul proclaims that salvation is also *anchored in the future* because God gives every one of His children the unchangeable promise that one day they will be clothed with the glory of His own Son. (We will explore that promise in more detail in the next chapter.)

Jesus Christ guarantees the believer's hope because He Himself is our hope (1 Tim. 1:1). In His beautiful high-priestly prayer, Jesus said to His Heavenly Father, "The glory which Thou hast given Me I have given to them; that they may be one, just as We are One" (John 17:22). We as believers don't earn our future glory in heaven but will receive it from God's gracious hand, just as we received redemption and sanctification.

In addition to exulting in our certain hope of the glory of God, we also have reason to exult in our tribulations because they contribute to a present blessing and ultimate glory. *Thlipsis* ("tribulations") has the underlying meaning of being under pressure and was used to describe squeezing olives to extract oil and squeezing grapes to extract juice.

Tribulation brings about perseverance; and perseverance, proven character; and proven character, hope; and that hope will not disappoint us in the end. Our afflictions for Christ's sake produce increasing levels of maturity in handling the trials of life. It should not seem strange then, that God's children are destined for affliction in this life (1 Thes. 3:3).

Our Heavenly Father increases and strengthens our "hope of the glory of God" (Rom. 5:2) through the process of tribulation, perseverance, and proven character—the end product of which is a hope that does not disappoint. In a sense, godly hope begets godly hope. The more believers pursue holiness out of hope for the final outcome, the more they will be persecuted and troubled, and the greater will be their hope as they see themselves sustained through it all by God's powerful grace.

Receiving a Unique Kind of Love

A fourth marvelous link in the unbreakable chain that eternally binds us as believers to Christ is our possession of the love of God, which "has been poured out within our hearts through the

Holy Spirit who was given to us. For while we were still helpless, at the right time Christ died for the ungodly. For one will hardly die for a righteous man; though perhaps for the good man someone would dare even to die. But God demonstrates His own love toward us, in that while we were yet sinners, Christ died for us" (Rom. 5:5-8). When a person receives salvation through Jesus Christ, he or she enters a spiritual love relationship with God that lasts throughout all eternity.

In verse 8, Paul makes it clear that "love of God" does not here refer to our love for God but to His love for us. The overwhelming truth of the Gospel is that God loved sinful, fallen, rebellious humanity so much "that He gave His only begotten Son, that whoever believes in Him should not perish, but have eternal life" (John 3:16). And, as Paul goes on to proclaim in Romans 5:9, since God loved us with so great a love before we were saved—when we were still His enemies—how much more does He love us now that we are His dear children!

Taking the truth of eternal security out of the objective area of the mind, Paul revealed that, in Christ, we are also given subjective evidence of permanent salvation. It is this evidence that God Himself implants within our deepest being: We love the One who first loved us (1 John 4:7-10; cf. 1 Cor. 16:22).

"Poured out" in Romans 5:5 refers to lavish outpouring to the point of overflowing. Our Heavenly Father doesn't proffer His love in measured drops but in immeasurable torrents. God's gift of His Holy Spirit to indwell believers is a marvelous testimony to His love for us, because He would hardly indwell those whom He did not love. And it is only because of the indwelling Spirit that His children are able to truly love Him. Speaking to His disciples about the Holy Spirit, Jesus said, "He who believes in Me, as the Scripture said, 'From his innermost being shall flow rivers of living water' " (John 7:38-39). Those rivers of blessing can flow out of us only because of the divine rivers of blessing, including the blessing of divine love, that God has poured into us.

Knowing we his readers would want to know more about the quality and character of the divine love that fills us, Paul reminds us of the greatest manifestation of God's love in all history, perhaps in all eternity: While we as ungodly sinners were utterly helpless to bring ourselves to God, He sent His only begotten Son, Jesus Christ, to die for us—notwithstanding the fact that we were completely unworthy of His love. When we were powerless to escape from our sin, powerless to escape death, powerless to resist Satan, and powerless to please Him in any way, God amazingly sent His Son to die on our behalf.

Natural human love is almost invariably based on the attractiveness of the object of love, and we are inclined to love people who love us. Consequently, we tend to attribute that same kind of love to God. We think that His love for us depends on how good we are or how much we love Him.

But God's immense love is supremely demonstrated by Christ's dying for the ungodly—for totally unrighteous, undeserving, and unlovable humanity. It is rare for a person to sacrifice his or her own life to save the life of someone of high character. Fewer still are inclined to give their lives to save a person they know to be a wicked scoundrel. But God was so inclined, and in that fact is our security and assurance. Saved, we can never be as wretched as we were before our conversion—and He loved us totally then.

Certain Deliverance

In Romans 5:9-10, Paul says, "Much more then, having now been justified by His blood, we shall be saved from the wrath of God through Him. For if while we were enemies, we were reconciled to God through the death of His Son, much more, having been reconciled, we shall be saved by His life." As if the first four were not enough to overwhelm us completely with assurance, there is a fifth link in the unbreakable chain that binds us to Christ: our certainty of deliverance from divine judgment.

Since God had the power and the will to redeem us in the

first place, how "much more then" does He have the power and the will to keep us redeemed? Not only did our Savior deliver us from sin and its judgment, but He also delivers us from uncertainty and doubt about that deliverance. Since God has already made sure of our rescue from sin, death, and future judgment, how can our present spiritual life possibly be in jeopardy? How can a Christian, whose past and future salvation are secured by God, be at risk during the time in between? Sin was no barrier to the beginning of our redemption, so how can it bar its completion? Since in its greatest degree sin could not prevent our becoming reconciled, how can it in any lesser degree prevent our staying reconciled? Since God's grace covers the sins of even His enemies, how much more does it cover the sins of His children!

Paul was reasoning from the greater to the lesser. It is a greater work of God to bring sinners to grace than to bring saints to glory. That's because sin is further from grace than grace is from glory. Therefore, rest in the promise of His glory.

Joy Inexpressible

"And not only this," Paul concluded, "but we also exult in God through our Lord Jesus Christ, through whom we have now received the reconciliation" (v. 11). A sixth and final link in the unbreakable chain that eternally binds us as believers to Christ is our joy or exultation in God. It may not be the most important or most profound evidence of our security in Christ, but it may be the most tender. And although this divine joy is subjective, it is nonetheless real.

Perhaps nowhere outside of Scripture has this deepest level of Christian joy been expressed more beautifully than in these stanzas from Charles Wesley's magnificent hymn "O for a Thousand Tongues to Sing":

O for a thousand tongues to sing
My great Redeemer's praise,

The glories of my God and King,
The triumphs of His grace!

Hear Him ye deaf; His praise, ye dumb,
Your loosened tongues employ;
Ye blind, behold your Savior come;
And leap ye lame for joy!

Because of these six links binding the believer to the Lord, there is true eternal salvation and every reason for full assurance of it.

FOUR

The Inevitable Glory

One of the links in the previous chapter's chain of assurance is the believer's exulting "in hope of the glory of God" (Rom. 5:2). Paul developed that theme further in a straightforward presentation of the doctrine of security in Romans 8. As we have seen, many texts in the Bible discuss the security of the believer, but none are as pointed as Romans 8:28-30. We find in those verses that everyone who has been redeemed by Jesus Christ—without exception—will be glorified.

The key phrase in this trilogy of verses is at the end of verse 28: "called according to His purpose." We as believers are forever secure because that is God's purpose. In verses 29-30, Paul carefully explains what God's purpose is: "For whom He foreknew, He also predestined to become conformed to the image of His Son, that He might be the first-born among many brethren; and whom He predestined, these He also called; and whom He called, these He also justified; and whom He justified, these He also glorified."

God causes all things to work out for the believer's good, "according to His purpose." There is no other way to explain why He does it other than that He simply wants to. God is completely sovereign: He is free to make whatever decisions He wants. And He sovereignly chooses for all things to work together for the good and glory of those He redeems. Nothing can change that.

Your Salvation Was a Sovereign Act of God

You are a Christian not because of something you did, but because of something God decided. The Book of Ephesians begins: "Blessed be the God and Father of our Lord Jesus Christ, who . . . chose us in Him before the foundation of the world, that we should be holy and blameless before Him" (1:3-4). God chose us and will make us holy. Ultimately, all sin will be overruled. It's another way of saying that all things work together for our ultimate good.

"He predestined us to adoption as sons through Jesus Christ to Himself, according to the kind intention of His will" (v. 5). God predetermined to make us His sons and daughters and planned that our salvation would lead to glorification. We are saved by God's plan and at the same time preserved for future glory. Our security, therefore, doesn't depend on our ability to stay saved, but on God's ability to keep His promise (Heb. 6:17-18).

In Ephesians 1:9, Paul says that God "made known to us the mystery of His will, according to His kind intention which He purposed in [Himself]." God purposed or swore by Himself, and as we saw in chapter 1, there is nothing or no one greater He can swear by (Heb. 6:13). Because He is absolutely perfect and will never violate His Word, we are assured of our security.

"Also," according to Ephesians 1:11, "we have obtained an inheritance, having been predestined according to His purpose who works [Gk., *energeō*] all things after the counsel of His will." God energizes all things according to His will, which includes your salvation. The Apostle John adds, "As many as received [Christ], to them He gave the right to become children of God, even to those who believe in His name; who were *born* not of blood, nor of the will of the flesh, nor of the will of man, but *of* God" (John 1:12-13, emphasis added). It is true that we have to respond to the Gospel message to be born again. We have to receive Christ and believe in Him (Acts 4:12). However, we are regenerated by the will of God. Our response is secondary to God's decision.

Much of contemporary evangelism leaves people thinking that salvation is predicated on their decision for Christ. Actually it is based on God's decision for them. That is the emphasis of Scripture. How in the world could a person make a decision for God on his or her own? After all, an unbeliever "does not accept the things of the Spirit of God; for they are foolishness to him, and he cannot understand them, because they are spiritually appraised" (1 Cor. 2:14). Also, "the god of this world [Satan] has blinded the minds of the unbelieving, that they might not see the light of the Gospel" (2 Cor. 4:4).

We all start off ignorant, in darkness, and dead in sin (Eph. 2:1). There is no way we can muster up enough of whatever it takes to turn around and accept Christ. God makes the first move in line with His eternal purpose.

The Awesome Purpose of God

What is the great end toward which God is working? That believers be "conformed to the image of His Son, that He might be the first-born among many brethren" (Rom. 8:29). Specifically, God planned for you to be saved in eternity past to be made like Christ. It is impossible for a person to become saved, yet never become like Christ by losing his salvation. God promised glorification; that is His eternal purpose. Heaven, the forgiveness of sin, and the gifts of love, joy, peace, and wisdom are only a part of the reality of salvation. The main reason God saved us was to conform us to the image of His Son. God is redeeming an eternally holy, Christlike, glorified community of people. When you became a Christian, the process of your being conformed to Christ began. That process must be fulfilled because that is God's holy purpose.

In Romans 8:17, Paul says that if we are children of God, we are "heirs also, heirs of God and fellow heirs with Christ, if indeed we suffer with Him in order that we may also be glorified with Him." We were made sons and daughters of God that we might be heirs. Our inheritance is to be like Christ and receive all that belongs to Him. In the meantime we will suffer as He suffered. The teaching that people can lose their salvation is contrary to God's purpose in salvation to conform us to Christ's image through suffering.

The Greek verb translated "to be conformed" in verse 29 means "to bring to the same form with." We will be made into the same form as Christ's form both bodily and spiritually.

In Philippians 3:21, Paul says the Lord "will transform the body of our humble state into conformity with the body of His glory." Our glorified bodies will be like Christ's, but I don't think that means we will all look alike. Every human being is different, but we have basically the same physiology: our bodies work in the same way, in the same environment, and by the same principles. Likewise, when we go to glory, we will receive glorious bodies that work in the same environment and by the same principles as the resurrected, glorified body of the Lord Jesus Christ.

We will also be like Christ spiritually. We will be perfect inwardly, not just outwardly. Residing in us will be the very holiness of Jesus Christ. The divine, incorruptible nature given to us at redemption will be freed from all that's holding it back in this fallen world.

We were predestined to be conformed "to the image of [God's] Son" (Rom. 8:29). The Greek word translated "image" (*eikōn*, from which comes the English word *icon*) refers to a statue made to look like someone or something. It is not an incidental or accidental likeness but a calculated, replicated image. We won't end up in the image of Christ accidentally; we'll be directly replicated in His image. That's what John had in mind when he said, "We know that, if He should appear, we shall be like Him, because we shall see Him just as He is" (1 John 3:2).

One of my favorite verses is 2 Corinthians 3:18: "We all, with unveiled face beholding as in a mirror the glory of the Lord, are being transformed into the same image from glory to glory, just as from the Lord, the Spirit." When you became a Christian, your spiritual eyes were opened and you started looking at the glory of the Lord. From there you are being progressively taken from one level of glory to the next; you are becoming more and more Christlike until the day you actually see Christ and become like Him. Truly God is forming you into the very image of His Son!

Here's the big picture: God created us so that there would be a group of people who would give Him the glory He deserves. A rebellion had begun in the Garden of Eden, yet God set out to redeem humanity. By His marvelous sovereign wisdom, He called rebellious humanity back to a place of giving Him glory. His goal in salvation is to bring believers to glory—to create an eternally redeemed community of people who are Christlike—and let Christ stand as the preeminent One, receiving worship and praise forever.

Now can you more fully appreciate why you were saved—and why therefore your salvation is secure? It wasn't just to keep you out of hell or to make you happy. The ultimate reason God is conforming you into Christ's image is so you will be able to give glory to the One who is most glorious.

That Christ is "the firstborn among many brethren" (Rom. 8:29) is a beautiful thought. Christ Himself calls us brothers and sisters (Heb. 2:11). He didn't have to do that. He could have made us His servants only. He didn't have to bring us into His family, but He did. Even though God wants us to glorify Him and His Son, He also desires intimacy with us.

God gives us joy, peace, and a future in heaven. Those are all elements of His grace to sinners. But it's not our happiness or our holiness that is the apex of His divine purpose—glorifying

His Son is. Christ is the central point of redemptive history—
not us. Therefore, if God saved you, He will certainly glorify you
to fulfill His purpose in bringing you to salvation. God's plans
cannot be thwarted. If they could, He wouldn't be God.

The Sure Progress of Salvation

There are five elements in God's wonderful process of bringing
you to glory:

Foreknowledge.

Romans 8:29 begins: "For whom He foreknew." That is where
the redemptive plan starts—with God's foreknowledge. Some
people have suggested that it is the same as foresight. They
envision God in heaven looking into the future with supernatural binoculars: That is, if He sees that you will believe in the
Gospel, they say He chooses you; if He sees that you won't, they
say He doesn't. Now it's true that God can see everything that
will happen in the future. He knows exactly what people will
do. But, if you claim that salvation is based merely on God's
foresight into the decisions of individual men and women, you
are actually claiming that people secure their own salvation.

Just believing that God knew who would and who would not
receive Christ as Savior and Lord does not explain how salvation starts with God's foreknowledge. Our finite minds have
difficulty understanding why people go to hell. We try to explain it by saying it isn't God's choice to send anyone to hell;
He just knows that some will choose to go that path. But, if
God knew certain people would end up in hell, why did He
bother creating them? You see, the main problem still remains
for those who would substitute "foreknowledge" with "foresight."

Also, if you claim that God merely knew what was going to
happen in the future, you still haven't explained how sinners
become saved. How can a person who is dead in sin, blinded by
Satan, unable to understand the things of God, and continuous-

ly filled with evil suddenly exercise saving faith? A corpse could sooner come out of a grave and walk!

Some have tried to answer that objection by asserting that, although everyone begins life with a sin nature, God restores each individual to the point of having the ability to believe. The Holy Spirit is said to lead the sinner step by step toward salvation if the sinner receives the Spirit's promptings. People, therefore, are left to their own devices to somehow muster up enough obedience to warrant the Spirit's ongoing involvement in their lives. That is clearly not biblical. In Ephesians 2:8-9, for example, Paul states, "By grace you have been saved through *faith*; and that *not of yourselves, it is the gift of God*; not as a result of works, that no one should boast" (emphasis added; cf. Rom. 3:19-20; Titus 3:5). Faith originates with God, not people.

The Book of Acts provides a good illustration of that truth: "When the Gentiles heard [Paul and Barnabas preach] . . . as many as had been appointed to eternal life believed" (13:48). Salvation is appointed, which means it inevitably ends in eternal life and glory. There is no salvation in which a person doesn't ultimately become conformed into the image of Christ for the purpose of exalting the preeminent One. In Acts 13, the reason the Gentiles believed is they were ordained to do so.

God's foreknowledge, therefore, is not a reference to His omniscient foresight but to His foreordination. God does indeed foresee who is going to be a believer, but the faith He foresees is the faith He Himself creates. It's not that He merely sees what will happen in the future; rather He ordains it. The Bible clearly teaches that God sovereignly chooses people to believe in Him. Peter's first epistle begins: "Peter, an apostle of Jesus Christ, to those who reside as aliens, scattered throughout Pontus, Galatia, Cappadocia, Asia, and Bithynia, who are chosen according to the foreknowledge of God the Father" (1 Peter 1:1-2). We too are chosen by God's foreknowledge or foreordination.

In addition to the idea of foreordination, the term *foreknowledge* also connotes a predetermined love relationship. That adds

an intimate tone to a biblical doctrine some find cold and hard
to accept. In the statement "Cain knew his wife; and she con-
ceived" (Gen. 4:17, KJV), we see knowledge and intimacy inter-
twined. The same word is translated "chosen" in Amos 3:2,
where the Lord said to Israel, "You only have I chosen of all the
families of the earth" (NIV). God "knew" Israel in the unique
sense of having predetermined that she would be His chosen
people. In the same sense God predetermined to love us.

Predestination.

The Greek word translated "predestined" in Romans 8 means
"to appoint" or "to mark out before." It is also used in Acts 4:
"There were gathered together against Thy holy Servant Jesus,
whom Thou didst anoint, both Herod and Pontius Pilate, along
with the Gentiles and the peoples of Israel, to do whatever Thy
hand and Thy purpose predestined to occur" (vv. 27-28).

The word *foreknowledge* is also used in reference to Christ's
crucifixion (Acts 2:23). That means foreknowledge and predestination must mean more than simple foresight into the future.
Otherwise, the Book of Acts would be saying God foresaw what
Jesus—on His own prerogative—was going to do and reacted to
it. That belief is clearly heretical. However, if we understand
foreknowledge and predestination to mean that God predetermined Christ's death to redeem humanity, then it follows that
He predetermined to redeem us.

Calling.

Romans 8:30 says that those whom God predestined, "He also
called." God's calling is where His eternal plan intersects with
your life. In eternity past, He predetermined to love you—He
predestined your salvation. God's calling begins when He moves
into your life on this earth, within the boundaries of time.

In addition, Paul says, "We know that God causes all things
to work together for good to those who love God, to those who
are called according to His purpose" (Rom. 8:28). "Called" re-

fers not to an outward call, but an inward one. It speaks of when God turns around a person's heart—a heart that could never turn to God, know Him, understand the Gospel, or know hope on its own. We know this refers to a saving call because of the context of Romans 8:30: "Whom He called, these He also justified; and whom He justified, these He also glorified." The calling here is an effectual call. It's not an invitation to just anyone; it's an invitation that will inevitably be received.

In 2 Timothy 1:9, Paul says God "has saved us, and called us with a holy calling, not according to our works, but according to His own purpose and grace which was granted us in Christ Jesus from all eternity." That ties in God's call with the security of our salvation: We were called to fulfill a purpose that was planned before God created the world. Since God planned that we be like Christ and exalt Him preeminently, He will fulfill it. We cannot lose our salvation; God continually overrules all things to fulfill His holy purpose, which involves our ultimate glorification.

God's call reaches us through the Gospel (2 Thes. 2:13-14), which convicts us of sin and draws us toward the Savior. It also comes through His grace. In Ephesians 1:6, Paul says we were chosen "to the praise of the glory of His grace." Whatever reason God had for choosing us, it was for Himself, not us. God's call is no reason for boasting (Eph. 2:8-9).

Justification.
To be justified is to be made right with God. How does that happen? The sin in your life must be removed. Specifically, God "has taken it out of the way, having nailed it to the cross" (Col. 2:14). When God called you to Himself by moving your heart to respond in faith to Christ, He applied Christ's payment for sin on your behalf. That satisfied God's righteous requirement, thus making you right with Him. Some people wonder how much time there is between God's calling and our justification. I don't know. It's like wondering how much time it takes for a bullet to

go through two back-to-back sheets of paper. The distinction between calling and justification is theological; there isn't necessarily a time lapse. You are called to be justified. The calling occurs when God moves to change your heart, and justification is the result.

Glorification.

Since God predetermined to love you, redeem you, call you away from your sin, and make you right through your faith in Christ, the next step is glorification. "Whom He justified," Paul concludes in Romans 8:30, "these He also glorified."

Did you notice that statement is in the past tense? Your glorification is so secure that God speaks of it in the same tense that He spoke of your salvation. And your salvation is so secure that He used the same tense to speak of your calling, justification, and predestination. In one great moment of eternal time— I know that's an enigma, but I can't express the thought any other way—God said all those things were done. The moment He predetermined to love you, your glorification was so secure that He could speak of it as if it had already happened. Your salvation couldn't be more secure!

The Guarantee of Glorification

You were saved for glory, and all things are working toward that end. God's inevitable purpose is to make you like Christ as part of a redeemed humanity over which Christ will be preeminent. You *will* glorify and praise Him forever. Before the world began, God predetermined to set His love upon you and foreordained your salvation. In time, He moved into your heart and called you away from your sin. He made you right with Himself through Jesus Christ, and He destined you for glory. That is the great basis of your eternal security.

Do you feel as if we've gone down deep and stayed down long in the things of God? I hope so. I hope you feel as if you've been treading on holy territory, for there's nothing more sublime than considering the end toward which our great God is working. To deny the security of salvation is to misunderstand God's purpose entirely.

PART TWO:
IS IT REAL?

How You Can Tell Whether
You Are Truly a Christian

FIVE

Eleven Tests from an Apostolic Expert

I n 1746, about six years after the Great Awakening, in which Jonathan Edwards was the primary instrument of God to preach the Gospel and bring about the greatest revival in American history thus far, Edwards wrote *A Treatise Concerning the Religious Affections*. He wrote it to deal with a problem not unlike one we face today: the matter of evidence for true conversion. Many people want the blessings of salvation, especially eternal security, but no more.

In the explosive drama of the Great Awakening, it seemed as though conversions were occurring in great numbers. However, it didn't take long to realize that some people claimed conversions that were not real. While various excesses and heightened emotional experiences were common, scores of people didn't demonstrate any evidence in their lives to verify their claim to know and love Jesus Christ, which led critics to attack the Great Awakening, contending it was nothing but a big emotional bath without any true conversions.

Thus, partly in defense of true conversion and partly to expose false conversion, Jonathan Edwards took up his pen. He came to this simple conclusion: The supreme proof of a true conversion is what he called "holy affections," which is a zeal for holy things and a longing after God and personal holiness. He made a careful distinction between saving versus common operations of the Holy Spirit. Saving operations obviously produce salvation. Common operations of the Holy Spirit, he said, "may sober, arrest and convict men, and may even bring them to what at first appears to be repentance and faith, yet these influences fall short of inward saving renewal" (Iain H. Murray, *Jonathan Edwards: A New Biography* [Carlisle, Pa.: The Banner of Truth Trust, 1987], p. 255).

How can you tell whether the Holy Spirit has performed a saving operation? As the principle evidence of life is motion, Edwards wrote, so the principle evidence of saving grace is holy practice (pp. 262–63). He said true salvation always produces an abiding change of nature in a true convert. Therefore, whenever holiness of life does not accompany a confession of conversion, it must be understood that this individual is not a Christian.

In the very year Edwards' treatise was published, popular teaching asserted that, to the contrary, the only real evidence of true salvation is a feeling based on an experience—usually the experience at the moment of the alleged conversion. That teaching introduces the prevalent but erroneous concept that a person's true spiritual state is known by a past experience rather than a present pursuit of holiness. Edwards flatly contradicted that notion: "Assurance is never to be enjoyed on the basis of a past experience. There is need of the present and continuing work of the Holy Spirit . . . [in] giving assurance" (p. 265). This is no esoteric theological debate: The substance of your assurance is at stake.

A number of New Testament writers, of course, were very concerned about this matter of true salvation, as was our Lord Jesus Himself. The Apostle John dedicated his first letter to the subject, stating his theme at the end: "These things I have written to you who believe in the name of the Son of God, in order that you may know that you have eternal life" (1 John 5:13). Throughout the letter is a series of tests to determine whether you possess eternal life. If you don't pass these tests, you'll know where you stand and what you need to do. If you do, you'll have reason to enjoy your eternal salvation with great assurance.

Have You Enjoyed Fellowship with Christ and the Father?

This is an essential element in true salvation and the first test John presented. Look with me at chapter 1, which begins: "We [John and his fellow apostles] have seen and bear witness and proclaim to you the eternal life, which was with the Father and was manifested to us—what we have seen and heard we proclaim to you also, that you also may have fellowship with us; and indeed our fellowship is with the Father, and with His Son Jesus Christ" (vv. 2-3). Obviously he was going beyond just the earthly acquaintance he had with Jesus because he had no such earthly acquaintance with the Father. Rather, he was presently enjoying communion with the living God and the living Christ.

Now at first you might be tempted to think, *Well, good for John*, but his was not an isolated experience. In 1 John 5:1, he says, "*Whoever* believes that Jesus is the Christ is born of God; and whoever loves the Father loves the child born of Him" (emphasis added). It is characteristic of any believer to love God and Christ. It is a sign of the holy affections Jonathan Edwards spoke of. A relationship with God is basic to salvation. It is what we as believers were called to. "God is faithful," Paul says, "through whom you were called into fellowship with His Son, Jesus Christ our Lord" (1 Cor. 1:9).

Paul described what that fellowship meant to him personally: "I have been crucified with Christ; and it is no longer I who live, but Christ lives in me; and the life which I now live in the flesh I live by faith in the Son of God, who loved me, and delivered Himself up for me" (Gal. 2:20). There's something very experiential about that truth—it's not just a cold fact that we as believers have divine life living in us; there's an experience to be enjoyed in knowing God intimately.

Jesus implied as much when He said, "I came that they might have life, and might have it abundantly" (John 10:10). If He had just said, "I came that you might have life," we could conclude He was talking only about His gracious provision of eternal life. By adding that life could be *abundant*, Jesus was moving into the dimension of experience. The Christian life is a rich life. We're meant to experience joy, peace, love, and purpose. When someone who's about to be baptized testifies about coming to Christ, you won't hear, "The fact is, folks, I'm saved, and I'm just here to announce that." Invariably the person will describe to you the feeling—the overwhelming sense of forgiveness and purpose in his or her life.

Here's a taste of the abundant life Scripture describes in terms of our fellowship with the Lord. The "God of all comfort" (2 Cor. 1:3); "the God of all grace" (1 Peter 5:10); the God who supplies all [our] needs according to His riches in Christ (Phil. 4:19); the God who leads us to speak to one another in psalms and hymns, and spiritual songs, singing and making melody in our hearts to Him (Eph. 5:19); the God to whom we cry "Abba! Father!" (Rom. 8:15) like little children to the daddy we adore; the God we draw near to in time of trouble (Heb. 4:16)—He *Himself* so greatly enriches us. Our fellowship with Him is the abundant life we experience.

Have you experienced communion with God and Christ? Have you sensed Their presence? Do you have a love for Them that draws you to Their presence? Have you experienced the sweet communion of prayer—the exhilarating joy of talking to the living God? Have you experienced the refreshing, almost overwhelming sense of grace that comes upon you when you discover a new truth in His Word? If you have, then you have experienced the fellowship of salvation.

Are You Sensitive to Sin?
Let's go back to chapter 1 of John's first epistle, to this declaration in verse 5: "This is the message which we have heard from

Him and announce to you, that God is light, and in Him there is no darkness at all." John was saying that the message the Lord sent to us is about Himself, specifically that He is absolutely sinless. The Greek text literally says there's not a single bit of darkness in Him. Therefore, "If we say that we have fellowship with Him and yet walk in the darkness, we lie and do not practice the truth" (v. 6).

Light and darkness do not coexist. One drives the other away. John went on to develop that theme: "If we walk in the light as He Himself is in the light, we have fellowship with one another, and the blood of Jesus His Son cleanses us from all sin. If we say that we have no sin, we are deceiving ourselves, and the truth is not in us. If we confess our sins, He is faithful and righteous to forgive us our sins and to cleanse us from all unrighteousness. If we say that we have not sinned, we make Him a liar, and His word is not in us" (vv. 7-10).

Some people make some pretty amazing claims that hold no water. They claim to have fellowship with God — to be Christians (v. 6), to have no sin (v. 8), and even to have never sinned (v. 10). They think they are walking in the light when actually they are walking in darkness. It is characteristic of unbelievers to be oblivious to the sins in their lives. The individuals mentioned in verse 8 are not dealing with their sins because they think they've reached a state where they have no sin. But they are deceiving themselves. Those mentioned in verse 10 have never even confessed or acknowledged sin. With that attitude they are in fact denigrating God because God says "*all* have sinned and fall short of the glory of God" (Rom. 3:23, emphasis added). Since unbelievers are so insensitive to the reality of their condition, human sinfulness is the right starting point in sharing the Gospel.

Believers, on the other hand, "walk in the light as He Himself is in the light" (v. 7). We walk a virtuous walk, and what's more, "we confess our sins" (v. 9). True believers have a right sense of sin. They know if they're going to commune with God,

they have to be holy. When sin occurs in their lives, they know
it must be confessed.

John takes this teaching a step further in the next chapter.
"My little children," he explained, "I'm writing these things to
you that you may not sin. And if anyone sins, we have an
Advocate with the Father, Jesus Christ the righteous" (v. 1).
True believers realize they don't have to sin. But when they do,
they know whom to go to—Jesus Christ, the believer's advocate.
As we explored in chapter 1, the intercessory work of Christ is
one of the great trinitarian securers of our salvation. That's an
encouraging reality to hang onto when confronted with personal
sin.

The person who is truly saved is sensitive to the sinful realities in his or her life. That's the example Paul left us in speaking
of his heightened awareness of sin's work in his own life (Rom.
7:14-25). Consider how that applies to you. Are you very much
aware of the spiritual battle raging within you? Do you realize
that to have true communion with God, you have to live a holy
life—that you can't walk in darkness and claim to have fellowship with Him? Are you willing to confess and forsake any sin in
your life as you become aware of it? Do you realize you can
choose not to sin—that you're not fighting a battle you're
obliged to lose? But when you do fail, do you go to your divine
Advocate? Do you sometimes cry out with Paul, "Wretched
man that I am! Who will set me free from the body of this
death?" (Rom. 7:24) because you're so weary of the burden of
sin in your flesh? If so, you are obviously a Christian. And since
salvation is secure, you might as well enjoy it and be fully
assured.

Do You Obey God's Word?

First John 2:3 couldn't be clearer: "By this we know that we
have come to know Him, if we keep His commandments." If
you want to know whether you're a true Christian, ask yourself
whether you obey the commandments of Scripture. That's how

Jesus described a true disciple when giving His Great Commission to go into all the world and make disciples (Matt. 28:20). Obedience to the commands of God produces assurance—the confidence of knowing for sure "that we have come to know Him." The Greek word translated "keep" in verse 3 speaks of watchful, careful, thoughtful obedience. It involves not only the act of obedience, but also the spirit of obedience—a willing, habitual safeguarding of the Word, not just in letter but in spirit. That's supported by the word translated "commandments," which refers specifically to the precepts of Christ rather than laws in general. Legal obedience demands perfection or penalty, while 1 John 2:3 is a call to gracious obedience because of the penalty Christ has already paid.

Verse 4 presents a logical contrast: "The one who says, 'I have come to know Him,' and does not keep His commandments, is a liar, and the truth is not in him." That person is making a false claim. "But whoever keeps His Word, in him the love of God has truly been perfected" (v. 5). How can you determine if you are a true Christian? Not by sentiment but by obedience.

If you desire to obey the Word out of gratitude for all Christ has done for you, and if you see that desire producing an overall pattern of obedience, you have passed an important test indicating the presence of saving faith.

Do You Reject This Evil World?

We now come to John's fourth test of what characterizes the true Christian: "Do not love the world, nor the things in the world. If anyone loves the world, the love of the Father is not in him" (1 John 2:15). This love speaks of our deepest constraints, our most compelling emotions and goals. Christians won't feel that way toward anything in this world because they know that until Christ returns, this world is dominated by God's enemy. John said, "We know that we are the children of God, and that the whole world is under the control of the evil one" (1 John 5:19, NIV). Satan, for now, is "the god of this world" (2 Cor. 4:4).

The evil one has designed a system that the Bible simply calls "the world." The Greek term *(kosmos)* speaks of a system en-compassing false religion, errant philosophy, crime, immorality, materialism, and the like. When you become a Christian, such things repel you, not attract you. Sometimes you may be lured into worldly things, but it isn't what you love; it's what you hate. That's the way Paul felt when he fell into sin (Rom. 7:15). As frustrating as it is to fall like that from time to time, we who are believers can be grateful that sin is something we hate and not love. That's because our new life in Christ plants within us love for God and the things of God.

"All that is in the world," John specified, "the lust of the flesh and the lust of the eyes and the boastful pride of life, is not from the Father, but is from the world. And the world is passing away, and also its lusts; but the one who does the will of God abides forever" (1 John 2:16-17). The world and its fleshly pre-occupations are but temporary realities. The true believer, in contrast, has eternal life and will abide forever.

Jesus said those who follow Him are not of the world just as He was not of the world. We still move about *in it* to do His will as long as we are alive, but we are not *of it.* That's why Jesus prayed specifically for the Father to keep us from the evil one (John 17:14-16). We're vulnerable to being sucked into this evil world's system now and then, but our love is toward God. That love is what will draw us out and redirect our focus toward heavenly priorities.

Do you reject the world? Do you reject its false religions, damning ideologies, godless living, and vain pursuits? Instead, do you love God, His truth, His kingdom, and all that He stands for? That doesn't come naturally to any man or woman because the human tendency is to love darkness rather than light to mask evil deeds (John 3:19-20). Unbelievers are of their father the devil, and want to do the desires of their father (John 8:44). If you reject the world and its devilish desires, that is an indica-tion of new life in Christ. And since that new life is forever, settle into it with an abiding sense of assurance.

Do You Eagerly Await Christ's Return?

Further along in 1 John, we come across a fifth test of salvation: "Beloved, now we are children of God, and it has not appeared as yet what we shall be. We know that, when He appears, we shall be like Him, because we shall see Him just as He is. And every one who has this hope fixed on Him purifies himself, just as He is pure" (3:2-3). If you're a true Christian, you will have hope in your heart, and your hope will be focused on Christ's return. That hope will purify your life.

Do you love Christ so much that you eagerly await to see Him face-to-face at His return and be made like Him? Scripture tells us that is the Christian's blessed hope and supreme joy. Romans 8 declares that the whole creation groans in anticipation of the glorious manifestation of the children of God. First John 3 says that it involves three things: Christ appears, we see Him, and we're instantly made like Him.

"Our citizenship is in heaven," Paul said, "from which also we eagerly wait for a Savior, the Lord Jesus Christ; who will transform the body of our humble state into conformity with the body of His glory, by the exertion of the power that He has even to subject all things to Himself" (Phil. 3:20-21). Are you waiting for that? Do you despise the sin in your fallen flesh and long to be like Christ? Can you feel the thrill of Paul's saying, "Just as we have borne the image of the earthly, we shall also bear the image of the heavenly"? (1 Cor. 15:49)

Such a hope has ethical power, for John said it purifies the one possessing it. Paul implied as much to Titus: "The grace of God has appeared, bringing salvation to all men, instructing us to deny ungodliness and worldly desires and to live sensibly, righteously, and godly in the present age, looking for the blessed hope and the appearing of the glory of our great God and Savior, Christ Jesus" (Titus 2:11-13). This is a sensible hope leading to sensible living. It is not an inordinate kind of anticipation where you are irresponsible with your earthly responsibilities. Being so heavenly minded that you're no earthly good is a contradiction in terms. The hope of Christlikeness will compel you to act more like Christ in reaching out to others and fulfilling all that God has set out for you to do.

If you find yourself longing for the return of Jesus Christ, that's evidence of salvation. It's an indication of a new nature within, which longs to be delivered from a body of sin while becoming like the perfect Christ. If you have such holy longings and affections, you've passed an important test indicating the reality of your eternal salvation.

Do You See a Decreasing Pattern of Sin in Your Life?

Another manifestation of holy affections is a decreasing pattern of sin. First John 3:4-10 spells out this sixth test:

> Every one who practices sin also practices lawlessness; and sin is lawlessness. And you know that [Christ] appeared in order to take away sins; and in Him there is no sin. No one who abides in Him sins; no one who sins has seen Him or knows Him. Little children, let no one deceive you; the one who practices righteousness is righteous, just as He is righteous; the one who practices sin is of the devil; for the devil has sinned from the beginning. The Son of God appeared for this purpose, that He might destroy the works of the devil. No one who is born of God practices sin, because His seed abides in him; and he cannot sin, because he is born of God. By this the children of God and the children of the devil are obvious: anyone who does not practice righteousness is not of God.

Unbroken patterns of sin are characteristic of the unregenerate. No matter what a person claims about being a Christian, if he or she continues in sin, it is only a claim and not a reality. When you became a Christian, the pattern of sin was broken and a new pattern came into existence. Holy affections took over. Does that mean there's no sin in your life? No, because your unredeemed flesh is still there. But the more you pursue those religious affections, the less you will sin.

Sin as a life pattern is incompatible with salvation. That's because to experience salvation is to be saved from something, and that something is sin. If a person could continue in sin after being saved from sin, that would mean salvation is ineffective. John therefore discussed the work of Christ to demonstrate just how effective it is.

He began by noting that there are people who practice sin and lawlessness (v. 4). Then Christ "appeared in order to take away sins" (v. 5). To say someone had the work of Christ applied to him or her, yet continues in the same pattern of sin is to deny the very purpose Christ came for, which was to take away sins. Continuing in sin is not consistent with Christ's work on the cross. If a saved person could keep on sinning, that would mean Christ's death—while having some efficacy in eternity—is in fact useless in time. Perish the thought! Christ's death served the very useful purpose of taking away not only the penalty of sin, but also the pattern of sin in the believer's life.

John went on to talk about Christ's work through the believer's union with Him: "No one who abides in Him sins" (v. 6). That cannot mean true Christians never sin because John just said, "If we say that we have no sin, we are deceiving ourselves, and the truth is not in us" (1:8). Rather, the next two verses in chapter 3 explain, "The one who practices righteousness is righteous, just as He is righteous; the one who practices sin is of the devil" (vv. 7-8). John's first epistle is consistent in warning against a *pattern* of sin.

Now let me clarify something here. I frequently receive letters from anguished Christians who doubt their salvation because they can't seem to break a sinful or unwise habit. They most often write about smoking, overeating, and masturbation. They fear their struggle with such things means they are locked into a

pattern of sin. But John is not saying that the frequent occur-
rence of one particular sin in a person's life means that person is
lost. Rather, he clarifies his meaning in saying that a true believer cannot practice lawlessness (1 John 3:4). The Greek term
used there (*anomia*) literally means living as if there were no
law. A person who rejects God's authority doesn't care what
God thinks about his habits, and is obviously not a Christian.

A Christian, however, has a drastically different way of relat-
ing to God. He or she is no longer a slave to sin, but has offered
himself or herself as a servant to the Lord (Rom. 6:14, 17-18). A
true Christian can still sin, and may even do so frequently, but
sinning frequently is not the same as *practicing sin*. In 1 John we
see that a true believer can do the first, but not the second.

Why is that the case? Because the true believer "abides in
Him" (1 John 3:6). Not only does Christ's death take away our
sin, but also His ongoing life in us breaks the sin pattern. No
longer are we perpetual sinners in thought, word, and deed—as
we were before we were saved. We now have the option to do
good. If we find ourselves sinning, contrary to the good we
desire to do inside, we are much like the Apostle Paul in Romans 7—and he's a great person to be associated with! Yet
because of the abiding presence of Christ, our struggle will de-
crease as time goes on. We will always be acutely sensitive to
sin, for as we have seen, that's one of John's tests of saving faith,
but it will be less of a pattern in our lives. Christ lives in union
with us to provide a new pattern—a pattern of righteousness.

A pattern of sin, however, signals a union with the devil:
"The one who practices sin is of the devil; for the devil has
sinned from the beginning. The Son of God appeared for this
purpose, that He might destroy the works of the devil" (v. 8).
The devil is a sinner and nothing but. Everyone who is associated with the devil is a sinner and nothing but. Christ came to
destroy the works of the devil by rescuing people who are in
bondage to sin. That means those who've really been rescued
will not continue in the state they've been rescued from. A

habitual pattern of sin indicates that a rescue has never taken place. To claim otherwise is to denigrate Christ by implying His death didn't accomplish what He set out to do—destroy the works of the devil by rescuing people from sin.

In addition, "No one who is born of God practices sin, because His seed abides in him; and he cannot sin, because he is born of God. By this the children of God and the children of the devil are obvious: any one who does not practice righteousness is not of God" (vv. 9-10). The believer has been born anew by the Holy Spirit. The seed He plants is a new nature, a new life principle, a new disposition. Just as a seed planted in the ground produces a distinct kind of life, God's seed produces a righteous life in us that breaks the pattern of sin. And don't worry: that seed cannot die, for the Word of God tells us it's imperishable (1 Peter 1:23). Born of the Spirit of God, the believer cannot continually sin.

John just provided us with four viewpoints in analyzing the sin in our life: the work Christ accomplished in His death, His ongoing life in the believer, His destruction of the devil's works, and the regenerating work of the Spirit. Every way you look at it, the pattern of habitual sin is broken. What does that mean to you personally? If you see a decreasing pattern of sin in your life, that's evidence of holy affections. The difference between the children of God and the children of the devil is, as John said, "obvious" (v. 10). If you practice righteousness, you're of God. If you don't, you're not. Plain and simple. If you see victory over sin in your life, if you see righteous motives, righteous desires, righteous words, righteous deeds, and if you're not all you ought to be but certainly not what you used to be, then you have eternal life, so enjoy it.

Do You Love Other Christians?

In 1 John 3:10, John mentions two obvious facts. One, as we just saw, is that "any one who does not practice righteousness is not of God." The other is that neither is anyone "who does not love his brother." To amplify that point, let's go back to a key section we missed in our progressive study of John's letter: "The one who says he is in the light and yet hates his brother is in the darkness until now. The one who loves his brother abides in the light and there is no cause for stumbling in him. But the one who hates his brother is in the darkness and walks in the darkness, and does not know where he is going because the darkness has blinded his eyes" (2:9-11).

To say you're in the light—or you've seen the light—is to claim to be a Christian. If so, your life would certainly show some of the life patterns of Christ. Loving fellow Christians is one very basic pattern. To be in fellowship with Christ is to experience and express love. If you claim to be a Christian but do not even like Christians, your claim is a sham. You are in fact walking in darkness, not in the light.

Loving fellow Christians comes naturally to the believer. As Paul said to the Thessalonian church, "[Regarding] the love of the brethren, you have no need for anyone to write to you, for you yourselves are taught by God to love one another" (1 Thes. 4:9). Nevertheless, he went on to encourage them to "excel still more" in their love for one another (v. 10). As believers, we haven't loved as fully as we ought to love, but we have loved. And we don't need to be taught to love because it's instinctive, implicit, and inherent within our new nature. As we learned in Romans 5:5, "The love of God has been poured out within our hearts."

Jesus went so far as to say, "By this all men will know that you are My disciples, if you have love for one another" (John 13:35). It is basic to our Christian life that we have the capacity to "fervently love one another from the heart," as Peter expressed it (1 Peter 1:22). And it's a love that goes beyond mere feeling to encompass dutiful responsibility, sacrificial service, and sensitive concern.

So here comes the test: Do you characteristically love other believers? If you claim to be a Christian but have no love in your heart for those in the church or any track record of meeting their needs, then the Apostle John says this to you: You're in the dark in spite of your claim to be in the light. Love is a test of divine life. It signifies you have crossed over from darkness to light. This is how 1 John 3:14-15 puts it: "We know that we have passed out of death into life, because we love the brethren. He who does not love abides in death. Everyone who hates his brother is a murderer; and you know that no murderer has eternal life abiding in him."

Do you honestly care about other believers or are you cold, uncaring, and indifferent? Do you have a desire to reach out and meet their needs? Those who don't care are spiritually dead, characterized by an ongoing hatred. In our sophisticated age, that is manifested not so much in vitriolic hostility as in an utterly self-centered approach to life. People who continually focus on themselves and couldn't care less what happens to anyone else are of their father the devil, who "was a murderer from the beginning" (John 8:44). As believers, however, "we know love by this, that [Christ] laid down His life for us"— quite the opposite of the devil's murderous character. Therefore, "We ought to lay down our lives for the brethren" (1 John 3:16).

John defined love as making sacrifices for others, perhaps even to the point of martyrdom. How do you respond to the opportunities you typically have to sacrifice your time, treasures, and talents? Are you happy when you come across a person or ministry in need, and you're able to provide money, time, prayer, a commodity, a skill, or a sympathetic ear?

What about enjoying the privilege of fellowship in general? Do you look forward to being with fellow Christians and talking with them, sharing with them, discussing the things of God with them, studying the Word with them, and praying with them? Do you have a desire to take the resources God has given you and apply them to someone else in the family of God? That's evidence of love, as John went on to explain: "Whoever has the world's goods, and beholds his brother in need and closes his heart against him, how does the love of God abide in him? Little children, let us not love with word or with tongue, but in deed and truth" (vv. 17-18).

Note the result of such a practical approach to love: "We shall know by this that we are of the truth, and shall assure our heart before Him, in whatever our heart condemns us; for God is greater than our heart, and knows all things. Beloved, if our heart does not condemn us, we have confidence before God" (vv. 19-21). The assurance that you are a Christian—that your faith is the real thing—will come by your love. The Greek word translated "assure" (peithō) means to pacify, tranquilize, soothe, or persuade. You can soothe yourself as you stand before God that you're a true Christian if you see love in your life.

Now your love won't be perfect, but it will be there. Let that bolster your assurance, for John warned that your heart or conscience may try to incriminate you and make you doubt. The fallen flesh has the capability to play games with your mind. Satan, the accuser of the brethren, may seek to exploit that tendency. In whatever your heart condemns you, you can be assured if you see love in your life. You may doubt your salvation, but God never does because He is greater than your heart and knows all things.

Perhaps you're going through doubt and struggling with your assurance. Do as John said and go back to the love of your life: Examine whether you love other Christians as evidenced by deeds of kindness and sacrifice. If that's characteristic of your life, be soothed, be pacified—for no matter what your heart may do to condemn you, you can be sure of your salvation. A condemning conscience can rob you of your assurance because it looks only at failure. But God is greater than your conscience; He looks at your faith in Christ.

The Apostle Peter, after denying Christ three times, had a worse time than any of us can imagine with a condemning heart. Jesus came personally to assure him. Three times in a row He inquired gently about Peter's devotion. In desperation, Peter replied, "Lord, You know all things; You know that I love You" (John 21:17). We too can appeal to the love God sees in our hearts. It's not perfect but, again, it's there. And it will express itself through deeds of kindness and sacrifice to others. Jesus told Peter to reveal his love by taking care of the church. It's natural for the Christian to "do good to all men, and especially to those who are of the household of the faith" (Gal. 6:10). Your love for fellow Christians is a benchmark of the Christian faith, and solid grounds for assurance. Refuse to let your heart condemn what God does not.

Do You Experience Answered Prayer?

Another source of confidence and assurance is this: Whatever we ask of God "we receive from Him, because we keep His commandments and do the things that are pleasing in His sight" (1 John 3:22). You can know you're a believer if God answers your prayers. The only way that can happen is if you keep His commandments, and the only way you can do that is if you belong to Him. As John says in verse 24, "The one who keeps His commandments abides in Him."

In a similar passage John said, "These things I have written to you who believe in the name of the Son of God, in order that you may know that you have eternal life. And this is the confidence which we have before Him, that, if we ask anything according to His will, He hears us. And if we know that He hears us in whatever we ask, we know that we have the requests which we have asked from Him" (5:13-15). God always answers prayers that are according to His will. Obedient believers know His will as stated in His Word, and tailor their prayers accordingly. The answers that result bring about confidence and assurance.

God is more eager to answer the prayers of His children than they are to ask. I suspect there's a certain disappointment in God's heart because He would do so much more than we ever ask Him to do. Think of the blessings and assurance we miss out on!

Now there are many people who pray to God, but don't even know the God they're praying to or what His will is. God is under no obligation to answer such prayers. We learn from the Psalms that He doesn't even hear them (cf. Ps. 66:18). But those of us who see answers to our prayers can know we have eternal life. One of the many good reasons to pray fervently and faithfully is to enjoy the assurance that answered prayer brings.

Some believers struggle with being assured of their salvation because they have scant experience concerning answered prayers. That comes from a skimpy prayer life. What a tragedy! If you're in that situation, reverse it immediately. I don't want you to miss out on the blessing and comfort that answered prayer brings. Looking back on my life, one of my greatest sources of assurance is seeing that God has answered many of my prayers through the years. That He answered is evidence that He hears me, which is evidence that I abide in Him and He in me.

Have you had your prayers answered? Is that a pattern of life for you? If so, you have eternal life. Have you prayed for an unbeliever and seen that person come to Christ? Have you prayed for someone in great distress and seen God turn the situation around into blessing and joy? Have you sought God about a void in your life and seen Him fill it? Have you prayed for forgiveness in a clear conscience and received it? Have you asked God to enable you to present His truth to an individual or group and experienced His grace to do so with great clarity? Have you sought power in proclaiming the Gospel and experienced it? Have you asked that God would help you lead someone to the Savior, and He did? Have you sought contentment amidst trying circumstances and experienced God's peace as a result? Have you asked the Lord to help you know Him better and experienced greater intimacy with Him after going through some hard lessons? Those are all indications that you belong to Him and He to you.

Do You Experience the Ministry of the Holy Spirit?

First John 4:13 develops that theme of belonging to God: "By this we know that we abide in Him and He in us, because He has given us of His Spirit." The first thing the Spirit did was "bear witness that the Father has sent the Son to be the Savior of the world" (v. 14). If you confess that Jesus is the Son of God, the Savior of the world, and have committed your life to Him, that was the Spirit's doing. Apart from the Holy Spirit, you wouldn't know who Christ is and you certainly wouldn't confess Him as Savior and Lord. Have you experienced that ministry of the Holy Spirit? If so, that's evidence of being a true child of God.

Another vital work of the Spirit is His illuminating your understanding of Scripture. John, speaking of the Spirit, said, "The anointing which you received from Him abides in you, and . . . teaches you about all things" (2:27). Paul explained that "the Spirit searches all things, even the depths of God . . . that we might know the things freely given to us by God" (1 Cor. 2:10, 12). When you read the Word of God, is its meaning illuminated to you? Do you understand what it says? In fact, do you sometimes understand it so well you wish you didn't understand quite that well because of the obvious implications? Is it relatively clear overall? Now I'm not talking about obscure passages that we all struggle with, but consider the effect that reading the Word has on you. Ask yourself, *Does it convict me when I'm sinful? Does it make me rejoice when I'm worshiping God and seeking to advance His kingdom?* Those are signs of the Spirit's illuminating work in your life.

Let's look at other ministries of the Spirit. What about fellowship with God? It is the Spirit who leads you to cry out "Abba! Father!" (Gal. 4:6) as a sign of your intimacy and communion with God. What about praise? Who is it that lifts your heart to praise and adore God? Who is it that compels you to sing with meaning and devotion? In Ephesians 5:19, Paul explains that the filling of the Spirit leads to "speaking to one another in

psalms and hymns and spiritual songs, singing and making melody with your heart to the Lord." What about the fruit of the
Spirit, which Paul describes as "love, joy, peace, patience, kindness, goodness, faithfulness, gentleness, [and] self-control"?
(Gal. 5:22-23) Those attitudes are spiritual graces. Have they
graced your life as a whole?

Have you ever ministered in a spiritual way through helping
someone, giving to someone, or speaking to someone about
Christ? Those are evidences of the Spirit of God. Do you actually experience His ministry in your life? In Romans 8:16, Paul
explains that "the Spirit Himself bears witness with our spirit
that we are children of God." Now don't expect Him to whisper
into your ear, "You're a Christian, you're a Christian, believe Me
you're a Christian!" There's no audible voice, nothing esoteric
or mystical, but something very concrete. He bears witness by
providing you with evidence of His presence in your life—by
illuminating Scripture to you, drawing you into fellowship with
God through prayer and praise, producing spiritual fruit to grace
your life, and enabling you to minister effectively to others.

If the Spirit is in your life, that's evidence that you abide in
God and He in you (1 John 4:13). So be assured. Don't let your
heart condemn you, damn you, tell you you're not a believer.
Recognize the Spirit's work in you. There's no reason to doubt
and be unstable.

Can You Discern between Spiritual Truth and Error?
So far we've taken nine tests for determining the presence of
saving faith. In the tenth is the one time John actually used the
word test: "Beloved, do not believe every spirit, but test the
spirits to see whether they are from God; because many false
prophets have gone out into the world. By this you know the
Spirit of God: every spirit that confesses that Jesus Christ has
come in the flesh is from God; and every spirit that does not
confess Jesus is not from God" (1 John 4:1-3).

Every false religious system in the world violates that test.

Adherents of such systems consistently attempt to undermine the biblical truth about who Jesus Christ is and what He accomplished—that He is Savior and Lord, who came in human flesh to be "delivered up because of our transgressions, and . . . raised because of our justification" (Rom. 4:25). Can you tell when someone is presenting false teaching about the person and work of Christ? That is the watershed issue of the Christian faith.

False teachers "are from the world; therefore they speak as from the world, and the world listens to them. We are from God; he who knows God listens to us; he who is not from God does not listen to us. By this we know the Spirit of Truth and the spirit of error" (1 John 4:5-6). John was saying a true believer will listen to the truth and not deviate into error about Christ's glorious person and work. Suppose someone says, "I used to believe in Jesus Christ, but now I've seen the light: Christ really was an angelic being—or an emanation from God, a divine spirit without the human element, or just a man and not divine." Any such heresies reflect an unregenerate heart.

From the moment of your salvation, there's one thing you're clear about and that's who Christ is and what He did, or you wouldn't be saved. It's the Holy Spirit who made that clear to you. This test is not moral or experiential but doctrinal. True believers know truth from error because the Spirit of Truth indwells them. "Whoever believes that Jesus is the Christ," John says, "is born of God" (1 John 5:1). That's the same doctrinal test again. When you believe the right thing about Christ, you're born of God.

It's good to be a believer, but it's also good to be skeptical. As John says, "Do not believe every spirit" (4:1, emphasis added). For the sake of your spiritual life and health, don't believe everything you hear, see, and read. Instead, "Test the spirits to see whether they are from God." That requires the ability to think biblically. The Greek text implies conducting a rigorous, ongoing examination of whatever and whomever you expose yourself to. Why go to all that trouble? "Because many false prophets have gone out into the world."

The conquering of the city of Troy is one of the most famous stories of antiquity. Greek soldiers had laid siege to the city for over ten years, but were unable to conquer it. In exasperation Ulysses, a brilliant strategist, decided to have a large wooden horse built and left outside the city walls as a supposed gift to the unconquerable Trojans. The Greeks then sailed away in apparent defeat. The curious and proud Trojans brought the wooden horse inside their fortified walls. That night Greek soldiers hidden inside the horse crept out and opened the city gates to let their fellow soldiers into the city. The soldiers massacred the inhabitants, looted the city, and burned it to the ground. Ever since, the Trojan horse has been a symbol of infiltration and deception. Throughout its history, the church has embraced many Trojan horses filled with false prophets.

Satan has effectively used enemies disguised as gifts to lure people away from the truth of God and into destructive error. Today's church is in a particularly severe state of confusion because of its weak doctrine, relativistic thinking, worldly methodology, inaccurate interpretation of Scripture, lax internal discipline, and spiritual immaturity. What is sorely needed is spiritual discernment—the skill of separating divine truth from error (1 Thes. 5:21).

Perhaps you are discerning in the everyday affairs of life. You read nutritional labels because you want to be healthy. You read the fine print of the stock market report before making financial investments. If you need surgery, you carefully select the right doctor. Maybe you're highly analytical about politics and can accurately assess a plethora of domestic and foreign issues. Or maybe you're an armchair quarterback who evaluates offensive and defensive strategies. All that is fine, but can you discern between divine truth and error?

To do that, John said to test for two things: confession of the divine Lord (1 John 4:2-3) and commitment to the divine Word (vv. 4-6). If you study the cults, you'll detect a pattern. Christian Science, Jehovah's Witnesses, Mormonism, and the like attack the person of Christ and then postulate a substitute or addition to the Bible, such as *Science and Health with Key to the Scriptures*, *The Book of Mormon*, or *The Pearl of Great Price*. True believers won't believe such lies. They have a resident truth teacher in the person of the Holy Spirit (1 John 2:27).

I listened to a radio program recently where a man was propagating a religion I never heard of before. It didn't take me long to discover he was not representing the truth. I was immediately put on guard by the way he skewed one brief biblical statement at the beginning of his message. I continued to listen rather intently until he was finished, whereupon he declared the existence of a great prophet who is the instrument of God to bring great truth to humanity. What he said did not square with Scripture. I knew it was error because the Spirit of God has convinced me about salvation by grace through faith in Christ alone and the veracity of Scripture. I knew I didn't need some prophet of modern times to give me the truth.

You don't have to be a seminary graduate or an expert on cults and world religions to distinguish truth from error. If you aren't swayed from the basic truths of Christ's divine person, work, and Word, that's evidence of genuine saving faith.

Have You Suffered Rejection Because of Your Faith?

This eleventh and last test is painful: "Do not marvel, brethren, if the world hates you" (1 John 3:13). Cain hated Abel and murdered him. Why did Cain do that? "Because his deeds were evil, and his brother's were righteous" (v. 12). Have you experienced animosity, hostility, rejection, bitterness, alienation, ostracism, prejudice, or outright persecution from representing and advocating what is right? If so, that's a sign that you belong to One who suffered the same way for the same reason.

The fact is, to the worldly, you as a Christian "have become as the scum of the world, the dregs of all things" (1 Cor. 4:13). You're a threat to their belief that this world is all that's worth living for. "They are surprised that you do not run with them into the same excess of dissipation, and they malign you" (1 Peter 4:4). However, Scripture says, "[Be] in no way alarmed by your opponents—which is a sign of destruction for them, but of salvation for you" (Phil. 1:28). When suffering on account of your faith, don't say, "Can I really be a Christian? Things are going so badly—I wonder if God cares." Rather, if the world is persecuting you, say, "Isn't this truly wonderful! It's pretty clear who I am."

I'll never forget one night several years ago when I was called to the church office to deal with an emergency. I arrived to find one of our elders struggling with a girl who was obviously demon possessed. She was evidencing supernatural strength. She flipped a heavy steel desk over onto its top and the two of us together were unable to restrain her physically. Voices that were not her own were speaking out of her. The first thing they said when I arrived was, "Not *him!* Get him out! Get him out! We don't want him here." It encouraged me to know that the demons knew I was not on their side.

That was a very confirming night for me. When the world and the spirit of Satan behind it come after you, you too have the right to be confirmed if you're hated because of righteousness. Now, if you're hated because you're obnoxious, there's no virtue in that! "But if when you do what is right and suffer for it you patiently endure it, this finds favor with God" (1 Peter 2:20). Part of that favor is being assured of your salvation.

The Apostle John gave all the tests that he did to give the true believer a biblical basis for confidence. Let's review his spiritual inventory: Do you enjoy fellowship with God and Christ? Are you sensitive to sin in your life? Do you obey the Scriptures? Do you reject this evil world? Do you love Christ and eagerly await His return? Do you see a decreasing pattern of sin in your life? Do you love other Christians? Do you receive answers to your prayers? Do you experience the ministry of the Holy Spirit? Can you discern between spiritual truth and error?

Have you suffered on account of your faith in Christ?

If you pass those tests, you can have confidence before God. After all, John wrote what he did so "you may know that you have eternal life" (5:13). There's no reason for you to go through your spiritual experience in the dumps, yet thousands of Christians do. Please don't be one of them.

PART THREE:
IS IT SOMETHING I CAN FEEL?

How You Can Experience
the Assurance of
a Secure Salvation

SIX

Dealing with Doubt

I n the introduction we noted that one reason people lack the assurance of their salvation is that many of them aren't saved. They have no scriptural basis for assurance. One of the reasons the Apostle John wrote his first letter was to help people in that position to realize that and do something about it. Let's now go beyond that issue. Why do so many *Christians* lack assurance? What about the thousands stuck in the spiritual dumps? There are eight basic reasons.

Strong Preaching
Some lack assurance because they are under strong preaching on God's holy standard. Such preaching forces people to see their sinfulness and acknowledge that the holiness of God calls them to a lofty standard of living.

Now that kind of preaching is both biblical and necessary. I want to emphasize that before going on to develop this theme. It is, in fact, woefully rare. Churches across our country are filled with smug people who don't feel particularly insecure because nothing in their life is ever confronted. Rather than leading their people to examine themselves and make sure their assurance is valid, many preachers feel it's their duty to make everyone feel good. But those who preach as they should will find some in their congregation plagued with doubt. Is that bad? No, the pulpit is rightly the creator of anxious hearts. How else can it unsettle those who have false assurance?

Unfortunately, however, a consistent call to righteousness may also unsettle some Christians—particularly those who are frequently succumbing to temptation. Remember the young man whose letter I shared with you at the beginning of this book? He felt like "a pile of manure on the white marble floor of Christ," painfully aware of his sinfulness because of doing the sin he didn't want to do and not doing the good he wanted to do. But he sounds more like Paul in Romans 7 than an unbeliever. The pulpit is supposed to create anxiety, but it should also give comfort and assurance to precious people like him who exalt Christ and desire to be more like Him. Good biblical preaching maintains that balance.

Guilt

Other Christians lack assurance because they have difficulty accepting the concept of forgiveness. They are often tyrannized by their emotions and feel they are too bad to be forgiven. There are several reasons for that. First, conscience speaks against forgiveness. The only thing your conscience knows about is guilt and conviction. It knows nothing of grace and mercy. Also, holiness and justice speak against forgiveness. They focus on sin and know nothing of excusing it.

Be warned: Satan is the accuser of the brethren. He will do all he can to obscure the love and graciousness of God. William Bridge wrote:

He that lacks assurance of God's love, converses too much with Satan. . . . [He says to himself:] "The devil is always following and tempting me to suspect the love of Christ, and he does it that he may attain his mind upon me. For the devil knows well enough that the more I suspect

Christ's love, the more I shall embrace Satan's love."

The truth is, beloved, this lack of assurance of God's love, or interest in Christ, is an inlet to many sins and miseries; for first a man doubts of his own salvation. Afterward he has continued doubting, then he rises up unto a full conclusion saying, "Now know I that Christ does not love me. I did but doubt before, but now I know He does not love me."

And after he has risen to this conclusion, then shortly he rises higher, and he goes further thus: "If Christ does not love me now, He will never love me; and if I have not an interest in Christ now, after all the preaching I have heard, and ordinances I have enjoyed, I shall never have it; and so the longer I live, the more I shall aggravate my condemnation" (*A Lifting Up for the Downcast* [Edinburgh: The Banner of Truth Trust, 1984 reprint], pp. 129–30).

Meanwhile, Thomas Brooks draws us back to Scripture:

Manasseh is saved. O despairing souls, the arms of mercy are open to receive a Manasseh, a monster, a devil incarnate; he caused that gospel prophet Isaiah to be sawed in the midst with a saw. . . . He turned aside from the Lord to commit idolatry, and caused his sons to pass through the fire, and dealt with familiar spirits, and made the streets of Jerusalem to overflow with innocent blood. . . . The soul of Mary Magdalene was full of devils; and yet Christ cast them out, and made her heart his house. . . . Why dost thou then say there is no hope for thee, O despairing soul?

Paul was full of rage against Christ and his people, and full of blasphemy and impiety, and yet behold, Paul is a chosen vessel, Paul is caught up into the heaven, and he is filled with the gifts and graces of the Holy [Spirit]. . . . Why should thou then say there is for thee no help, O despairing soul! . . . The apostle tells you of some mon-

strous miscreants that were unrighteous, fornicators, idol-
aters, adulterers, effeminate, abusers of themselves with
mankind, thieves, covetous, drunkards, revilers, extortion-
ers; and yet these monsters of mankind, through the infinite goodness and free grace of God, are washed from the
filth and guilt of their sins, and justified by the righteousness of Christ, and sanctified by the Spirit of Christ, and
decked and adorned with the precious graces of
Christ. . . .

Why then, O despairing soul, shouldst thou fear that thy
unworthiness and unfitness for mercy will so stop and turn
the stream of mercy, as that thou must perish eternally for
want of one drop of special grace and mercy? (*Heaven on
Earth: A Treatise on Christian Assurance* [Edinburgh: The
Banner of Truth Trust, 1982 reprint], pp. 93–94)

If you allow Satan to crush your head with the holy require-
ments of God stripped of the love of God, you will doubt.

Ignorance

Many people lack assurance because they do not understand
that salvation is an utterly divine, totally sovereign operation.
Assurance is built on the historical reality of what Jesus Christ
accomplished. It is not a feeling without reason, and you will
never have the *subjective feeling* of assurance until you compre-
hend the *objective truth* of the Gospel.

You must realize that God knew you were a sinner, which is
why He sent His Son Jesus Christ into the world to pay the
price completely for all your sins—past, present, and future. By
His omnipotent power God secured forever the salvation Jesus
offered.

It is irreversible. As Paul says, "The gifts and the calling of
God are irrevocable" (Rom. 11:29).

"Come now, and let us reason together," says the Lord engag-
ingly. "Though your sins are as scarlet, they will be as white as

snow; though they are red like crimson, they will be like wool" (Isa. 1:18). When God forgives you, it is complete. He Himself said, "I, even I, am the One who wipes out your transgressions for My own sake; and I will not remember your sins" (43:25). Does that sound like good news to you? What you can't forget, God can't remember! H.A. Ironside remarked, "You may never be able to forget the years of wandering, the many sins of which you have been guilty. But that which gives peace is the knowledge that God will never recall them again. He has blotted them from the book of His remembrance, and He has done it in righteousness, for the account is completely settled. The debt is paid" (*Full Assurance: A Series of Messages for Anxious Souls* [New York: Loizeaux Bros., 1937], p. 23).

When Israel was preparing to leave Egypt, the last plague, the death of the firstborn, was about to fall on the land. God instructed His people to slay a lamb and sprinkle its blood on the front door of their houses. The angel of death passed over every blood-sprinkled house. Inside the house some might have worried about sins they had committed, but their security depended not on their frame of mind, their feelings, or the record of their past deeds, but on the blood.

So it is today. We can't see the blood shed on Calvary for our redemption, but God does. He doesn't look at the believer and say, "Hey, he cheated"—or lied, or lacked kindness, or acted like a hypocrite. Your security from divine judgment doesn't depend on living a perfect life but on being sheltered by the blood of Christ.

Now there's one element of Gospel truth I want to mention specifically because of its major role in the issue of assurance: the resurrection of Jesus Christ. It proves that the Lord's work on the cross brought about a salvation that's eternally secure. There could have been no better attestation to the truthfulness of His claims. Jesus said He was God, and rose from the dead to prove it. He said He came to accomplish the work of salvation, and God raised Him from the dead to show He was successful.

Jesus Christ bore all the sins of all humanity in His body on the cross. Afterward God "raised Him from the dead, and seated Him at His right hand in the heavenly places" (Eph. 1:20). A new believer wisely reasoned, "If anyone is ever to be kept out of heaven for my sins, it will have to be Jesus, for He took them all upon Himself and made Himself responsible for them. But He is in heaven already, never to be turned out, so now I know that I am secure" (Ironside, p. 75). The matter is settled for those of us who trust in Christ. God "has saved us, and called us with a holy calling, not according to our works, but according to His own purpose and grace which was granted us in Christ Jesus from all eternity, but now has been revealed by the appearing of our Savior Christ Jesus, who abolished death, and brought life and immortality to light through the Gospel" (2 Tim. 1:9-10).

Assurance is an inextricable part of saving faith. As the Apostle John said it, "I have written to you who believe in the name of the Son of God, in order that you may *know* that you have eternal life" (1 John 5:13, emphasis added). The Christian faith is a secure faith. As a famous hymn triumphantly declares, "How firm a foundation, ye saints of the Lord, is laid for your faith in His excellent Word."

Uncertainty

Some Christians lack assurance because they don't know the exact time of their salvation. They can't remember when they believed. Some can't remember ever not believing. Because they can't pinpoint the exact moment, they doubt whether the moment actually occurred. But if you didn't know the date of your birth, you wouldn't wonder whether you were alive! Far too much has been made of isolating the moment by some formula, whether it be praying a prayer, signing a card, raising your hand, or walking down an aisle.

Many Christians, especially those raised in a Christian environment, can't identify the exact moment they were saved. I can't. I don't know when I passed from death to life, but I know that I did. There were times as a little child when I prayed special prayers. I specifically remember praying with my father on the steps of a church in Indiana when he was holding a revival meeting. His sermon convicted me because I had done some bad things that week—like trashing the schoolroom of the church. I remember as a 14-year-old going forward at camp and throwing a pine cone in the fire, teary-eyed and wanting to make my life right with God. I was in a serious auto accident when I was a freshman in college that vividly reinforced God's claim on my life, but I can't say for sure that was the time of my salvation.

I don't look for a past event to make my salvation real to me. I look at the present pattern of my life. Some people have a false assurance because they can remember a past event, but their life doesn't follow a righteous pattern. So don't worry if you can't relate a specific time or event to the moment of your salvation. Focus on your lifestyle and attitudes instead.

Temptation

Another reason many Christians lack assurance is they feel the pull of their unredeemed flesh and wonder whether they really have a new nature. As Christians who dwell in this fallen world, we are new creations incarcerated in unredeemed flesh. In fact we "groan within ourselves, waiting eagerly for . . . the redemption of our body" at our Lord's return, when it "will be set free from its slavery to corruption into the freedom of the glory of the children of God" (Rom. 8:23, 21).

But until that day of liberation comes, we will occasionally be drawn into the Romans 7 battle between flesh and spirit, doing what we don't want to do and not doing what we want to do. If sin is overwhelming and overpowering you at any given point, you will lack assurance. You'll wonder, *Did I repent enough? Am I sorry enough for my sin? Do I have enough faith?*

It's easy to read Romans 7 in an imbalanced way. If you focus only on the parts that say, "Nothing good dwells in me" and "wretched man that I am," you'll become overly introspective. Focusing on the flesh will warp your perspective and lead you to be overly negative about your spiritual condition. However, if you focus only on the parts that say, "I joyfully concur with the Law of God in the inner man" and "the wishing [of doing good] is present in me," you'll fail to deal with the reality of the flesh.

You need to keep a balance. Here's a helpful suggestion:

Test yourself in this way. You once lived in sin and loved it. Do you now desire deliverance from it? You were once self-confident and trusting in your own fancied goodness. Do you now judge yourself as a sinner before God? You once sought to hide from God and rebelled against His authority. Do you now look up to Him, desiring to know Him, and to yield yourself to Him? If you can honestly say "Yes" to these questions, you have repented. . . . And remember, it is not the amount of repentance that counts: it is the fact that you turn from self to God that puts you in the place where His grace avails through Jesus Christ.

Strictly speaking, not one of us has ever repented enough. None of us has realized the enormity of our guilt as God sees it. But when we judge ourselves and trust the Saviour whom He has provided, we are saved through His merits. As recipients of His lovingkindness, repentance will be deepened and will continue day by day, as we learn more and more of His infinite worth and our own unworthiness (Ironside, p. 89).

Do you see the impulses of the new nature in your life? If so, that's indicative of salvation. If God's will has become your highest joy, and submission to His lordship your greatest delight, you are indeed a child of God—no matter how strong the pull of sin.

Trials

Some Christians become spiritually unstable because they can't see the hand of God in all their trials. They say things like, "How could God love me and let me go through this? How could He take my husband—or wife or child? How could He not hear my prayer and deliver me? Where is God when I need Him?" People who think like that not only sentence themselves to doubt, but also miss what is actually the strongest source of assurance—proven faith.

Remember Romans 5? "Having been justified by faith, we have peace with God through our Lord Jesus Christ . . . and we exult in hope of the glory of God. And not only this, but we also exult in our tribulations; knowing that tribulation brings about perseverance; and perseverance, proven character; and proven character, hope; and hope does not disappoint" (vv. 1-5). We're to rejoice in our trials because they produce hope and assurance.

"Consider it all joy," James says, "when you encounter various trials, knowing that the testing of your faith produces endurance. And let endurance have its perfect result, that you may be perfect and complete, lacking in nothing" (1:2-4). Rather than causing you to doubt, the trials of life are meant to be divine demonstrations of God's love and power on your behalf as He helps you get through them all.

Through all you must endure in life, remember this: "God is not unjust so as to forget your work and the love which you have shown toward His name, in having ministered and in still ministering to the saints. [Therefore] show the same diligence so as to realize *the full assurance of hope* until the end, that you may not be sluggish, but imitators of those who through faith and patience inherit the promises" (Heb. 6:10-12, emphasis added). Handle your difficulties by being diligent and patient. The reward is a full assurance of hope.

Trials are the crucible in which assurance is formed. Remember Paul's great statement that nothing can separate us from the love of God? Note the context of his assurance: "Who

shall separate us from the love of Christ? Shall tribulation, or
distress, or persecution, or famine, or nakedness, or peril, or
sword? Just as it is written, 'For Thy sake we are being put to
death all day long; we were considered as sheep to be slaugh-
tered' " (Rom. 8:35-36). Paul had experienced all that and
more—take a good look at his autobiography in 2 Corinthians
11 sometime—yet he was certain of his relationship with God.
What convinces you of your salvation? Hopefully, it's the Word
of God and your tested faith.

Fleshliness

One of the most important ways the Holy Spirit ministers to
believers is by assuring them of their salvation. A believer who's
not living by the Spirit's power forfeits that important ministry.
Let's look again at Romans 8:15: "You have not received a spirit
of slavery leading to fear again, but you have received a spirit of
adoption as sons by which we cry out, 'Abba! Father,' " the
Aramaic equivalent of Daddy. We have been adopted into
God's family and are on intimate terms with Him. How do we
know that's true? Because "the Spirit Himself bears witness with
our spirit that we are children of God, and if children, heirs also,
heirs of God and fellow heirs with Christ" (vv. 16-17).

In Rome it was very common to adopt, and each adoption
had to be verified by seven witnesses. That policy was to insure
someone would be around to confirm the legitimate claim of the
heir to his or her inheritance. Now, if anyone questions your
claim to your eternal inheritance, there is a witness who was
present at the moment of your adoption: the Holy Spirit, whom
Isaiah 11:2 describes as the sevenfold Spirit. He will step forward and bear witness that you are indeed an adopted child of
God and have a lawful claim to an eternal inheritance.

How does the Holy Spirit bear witness that you are God's
child? In a number of ways, some of which we touched on in the
previous chapter. The first is by illuminating Scripture so you
can understand it. In 1 Corinthians 2:9-10, Paul says, "It is

written, 'Things which eye has not seen and ear has not heard, and which have not entered the heart of man, all that God has prepared for those who love Him.' For to us God revealed them through the Spirit." As you study the Word of God about those promises, the Spirit will make them real to you.

The second way the Spirit bears witness is through salvation. As we noted before, the Apostle John wrote, "By this we know that we abide in Him and He in us, because He has given us of His Spirit. And we have beheld and bear witness that the Father has sent the Son to be the Savior of the world. Whoever confesses that Jesus is the Son of God, God abides in him, and he in God" (1 John 4:13-15).

Another way in which the Spirit bears witness is by drawing you into communion with God. "Because you are sons," Paul says, "God has sent forth the Spirit of His Son into our hearts, crying, 'Abba! Father!' " (Gal. 4:6) The Spirit produces prayer, praise, and worship—a crying out to God as your Heavenly Father.

Yet another way He bears witness is the spiritual fruit He produces in you: "love, joy, peace, patience, kindness, goodness, faithfulness, gentleness, self-control" (Gal. 5:22-23). The flesh certainly doesn't produce those things. It knows lust, but not true love. It knows momentary happiness, but not settled joy. It knows a moment of calm, but not a deep inner peace. The fruit of the Spirit is evidence that you belong to God. So is the outworking of His mighty power in you through evangelism and other Christian ministries (cf. Acts 1:8).

Finally, Thomas Brooks' remarks conclude the matter: "The Spirit is the great revealer of the Father's secrets, he lies in the bosom of the Father, he knows every name that is written in the book of life; he is best acquainted with the inward workings of the heart of God toward poor sinners; he is the great comforter and the only sealer up of souls to the day of redemption. *If you grieve by your wilful sinning he that alone can gladden you, who then will make you glad?*" (*Heaven on Earth*, p. 152, emphasis added) If you grieve or quench the Spirit by walking in the flesh, you short-circuit His ministries to you and will lack assurance as a result.

Disobedience

Perhaps the most obvious reason for lacking assurance is disobedience, because assurance is the reward for obedience. The writer of Hebrews 10:22 makes that strong connection: "Let us draw near with a sincere heart in full assurance of faith, having our hearts sprinkled clean from an evil conscience, and our body washed with pure water." It's been well said that high degrees of assurance cannot be enjoyed by those who persist in low levels of obedience. To live in sin is to live in doubt.

Listen to the testimony of Charles Spurgeon:

> Whenever I feel that I have sinned and desire to overcome that sin for the future, the devil at the same time comes to me and whispers, "How can you be a pardoned person and accepted with God while you still sin in this way?" If I listen to this I drop into despondency, and if I continued in that state I should fall into despair, and should commit sin more frequently than before; but God's grace comes in and says to my soul, "Thou hast sinned; but did not Christ come to save sinners? Thou art not saved because thou art righteous; for Christ died for the ungodly." And my faith says, "Though I have sinned, I have an advocate with the Father, Jesus Christ the righteous, and though I am guilty, yet by grace I am saved and I am a child of God still." And what then? Why the tears begin to flow and I say, "How could I ever sin against my God who has been so good to me? Now I will overcome that sin," and I get strong to fight with sin through the conviction that I am God's child (source unknown).

Here's a practical way of dealing with sin: Eliminate a major sin in your life and the rest will follow. When the general is killed, the troops scatter. Think of what happened when David killed Goliath. By the means of grace available to you as a believer, slay the sins you find most compelling and familiar—your pet sins—and the others will soon disappear. And when you fall into sin, quickly set out to conquer that sin and be aware that Satan will try to make you doubt your salvation. Fall back on the forgiving grace of God, and it will strengthen you for battle.

A Practical Exercise

If you're lacking assurance—if you're plagued with doubts, have lost your joy, become useless in Christian service, empty in worship, cold in praise, passionless in prayer, and vulnerable to false teachers—whatever the problem, know there is a cure: obeying God's Word in the power of the Spirit.

Take a practical step now by applying an ancient technique to help you think through what God's Word teaches about assurance. It's a question-and-answer process known as a catechism—the Greek word *katacheō* means "to echo back." So echo back God's truth as you slowly and thoughtfully read the following out loud (partially adapted from Puritan William Guthrie's *The Christian's Great Interest* [Edinburgh: The Banner of Truth Trust, 1982], pp. 193–96):

Question: *What is the essential duty a person has in this world?* Consummating a saving relationship with the Lord Jesus Christ, which is to recognize His work on the cross and His resurrection from the dead as the satisfying atonement for sin, and walking in accord with that relationship.

Question: *Do all members of the church have a saving relationship with the Lord Jesus Christ?* No, only those who are truly saved.

Question: *How can I be certain I have that saving relationship?* The Lord will have done in your soul His own sovereign will—

that of calling you to Himself through a work of conviction and humiliation so you will have discovered your sin and misery, and being so seriously agitated and threatened by it, you long for the Savior.

Question: *How can I know if I've made sufficient discovery and admission of my sin?* By taking salvation to your heart above any other pursuit in life. It will make Christ, your Redeemer, very precious to your soul. It will make you fear sin, repent, and seek to be saved on God's terms.

Question: *What is another way of discerning a saving relationship to Christ?* A strong and serious affection that reaches toward Christ as He is progressively revealed to you in the Gospel. Such love is the product of saving belief.

Question: *Are there other marks of a relationship with Christ?* You are truly saved when you have been made a whole new person, graciously changed and renewed. That is best evidenced by a desire to shun sin and pattern your life in obedience toward God's righteous demands.

Question: *What if I find sin prevailing over me?* Although every sin deserves eternal vengeance, if you regularly confess your sins with unfeigned repentance and shame before God—fleeing to Christ for forgiveness for all known and unknown iniquities— He will grant you mercy and pardon because you stand in grace, and your salvation is forever secure.

Question: *What if my sins are serious and repeated?* Whatever they are, Jesus Christ has paid the price for them so that if you sincerely and earnestly have turned to Him in repentant faith, you will never enter into condemnation. Moreover, His gracious provision for those who believe includes power to overcome sin and live righteously.

Question: *Is faith alone the requirement for salvation?* Yes, it is the only basis upon which God offers peace and pardon to humanity. However, faith—if it is genuine—will not be alone in the soul, but will always be accompanied by true repentance and an eager desire to conform to God's will and way.

Question: *How can I be sure I've settled my eternal destiny with the Lord?* Express with your mouth to God what the Holy Spirit through Scripture has led you to believe in your heart.

Question: *What are the results of a relationship with Christ?* Union and communion with God here, and blessed fellowship and glory hereafter.

Question: *How can I come to full assurance that I have such a relationship?* By affirming the promises of God as revealed in Scripture by the internal witness of the Spirit, and by manifesting real and righteous fruit born out of love for Christ and a desire to bring Him honor and glory.

SEVEN

Adding Virtue upon Virtue

I n the summer of 1980 I took a three-month sabbatical from Grace Church. When I set out, I had the feeling that I might not be coming back.

I had been ministering at the church for over eleven years. That's a long time by comparison: I've heard that the average pastor in the United States spends just two years at any one church! I remember feeling I had taught my congregation everything I knew. I feared boring them by going over the same old things.

But during my sabbatical, the Lord redefined my priorities and reaffirmed His call to my ministry at Grace Church. I got a second wind that summer. I came back with renewed vigor and excitement about the church and the work of God.

What happened? The Lord taught me the importance of being used to remind believers of truth they already know. I sensed a new commitment and perspective in ministry based on my reading of 2 Peter 1. I really became excited when I realized the Lord had called Peter to do the same thing He was calling me to do.

This is what Peter said to his church: "I shall always be ready to remind you of these things, even though you already know them, and have been established in the truth which is present with you. And I consider it right, as long as I am in this earthly dwelling, to stir you up by way of reminder, knowing that the laying aside of my earthly dwelling is imminent, as also our Lord Jesus Christ has made clear to me. And I will also be diligent that at any time after my departure you may be able to call these things to mind" (vv. 12-15). I've been at my church for twenty-three years now. If I have my way, I'll be around a lot longer than that, reinforcing the truth just as Peter did.

God calls many individuals to that task, and there's good reason: It's incredibly easy to forget spiritual truth. That's what brought disaster to the nation of Israel. Early in its history, God told the people He feared that once they entered the Promised Land, they would forget Him (Deut. 8:14). And that's exactly what happened.

Remembrance

Remembrance is a vital aspect of Christian ministry. Celebrating Communion at the Lord's Table is a prime example—its point is that we might forever remember Jesus Christ and His sacrifice on our behalf. It challenges us to overcome the indifference bred by familiarity.

God has endowed the human brain with the capacity to reinforce spiritual truth. When you continually feed on the Word of God, you will respond in a spiritual manner almost involuntarily. When you do so, your brain becomes your friend. But your brain will be your enemy when you dwell on things that aren't pure.

Thomas Fuller, a minister from the previous century, wrote vividly of that reality. Perhaps you can relate to his struggle: "Almost twenty years ago I heard a profane jest and still I remember it. How many pious passages of far later date have I utterly forgotten? It seems my soul is like a filthy pond where fish die soon and frogs live long. Lord, raise this profane jest out of my memory. Leave not a letter thereof behind lest my corruption seek it out again. And, Lord, be pleased to write some pious meditation in the place thereof and grant, Lord, for the time to come that I may be careful not to admit what I find so difficult to expel" (source unknown). That was a good prayer. Scripture warns us to guard our hearts and minds (Prov. 4:23-27) because it's all too easy to remember the bad and forget the good.

That's why the Lord called Peter to a ministry of remembrance, and why He still calls ministers to the same purpose today. Peter said, "I shall always be ready to remind you of *these things*" (2 Peter 1:12, emphasis added). What things? What is so important for us to remember? What Peter just finished talking about in verses 1-11. The passage reads as follows:

> Simon Peter, a bondservant and apostle of Jesus Christ, to those who have received a faith of the same kind as ours, by the righteousness of our God and Savior, Jesus Christ: Grace and peace be multiplied to you in the knowledge of God and of Jesus our Lord; seeing that His divine power has granted to us everything pertaining to life and godliness, through the true knowledge of Him who called us by His own glory and excellence. For by these He has granted to us His precious and magnificent promises, in order that by them you might become partakers of the divine nature, having escaped the corruption that is in the world by lust.
>
> Now for this very reason also, applying all diligence, in your faith supply moral excellence, and in your moral excellence, knowledge; and in your knowledge, self-control, and in your self-control, perseverance, and in your perseverance, godliness; and in your godliness, brotherly kindness, and in your brotherly kindness, love. For if these qualities are yours and are increasing, they render you neither useless nor unfruitful in the true knowledge of our Lord Jesus Christ.
>
> For he who lacks these qualities is blind or short-sighted, having forgotten his purification from his former sins.

Therefore, brethren, be all the more diligent to make certain about His calling and choosing you; for as long as you practice these things, you will never stumble; for in this way the entrance into the eternal kingdom of our Lord and Savior Jesus Christ will be abundantly supplied to you.

Peter was very concerned that his readers enjoy assurance. That's why he began his second letter with this discourse on salvation. Understanding it is crucial for dealing with false teachers, whom Peter warned against in the rest of the letter.

Experts tell us that perhaps the most exploited victims of cults are insecure Christians who consistently doubt their salvation. False teachers have ways of making them miserable and confused. But to those who are confident in their salvation—confident in the spiritual riches Christ has endowed them with, secure and assured in their true knowledge of the Savior—false teachers have nothing to offer.

In 2 Peter 1:1, Peter mentions the source of salvation: "the righteousness of our God and Savior, Jesus Christ." In verse 2, he specifies the substance of our salvation, which is predicated on multiplied grace. In verses 3-4, he describes the sufficiency of our salvation: we have "everything pertaining to life and godliness."

And in verses 5-11, he proclaims the certainty of our salvation. That certainty is the result of putting all the spiritual resources we have to good use by adding virtue upon virtue.

Diligence
With verse 5 the virtue list starts off by indicating we're to apply all diligence. Now that may come as a surprise after hearing in verses 3-4 about all the good things God has already done for us. You might expect the next statement to be, "So let go and let God. Relax and wait for Him to do it all." Hardly. Peter said to expend maximum effort to equip or supply ourselves (Gk., *epichorēgein*) with a series of virtues. William Barclay explained:

[That Greek verb] comes from the noun *chorēgos*, which literally means *the leader of a chorus*. Perhaps the greatest gift that Greece and especially Athens, gave to the world was the great works of men like Aeschylus, Sophocles and Euripides, which are still among its most cherished possessions. All these plays needed large choruses and were, therefore, very expensive to produce.

In the great days of Athens there were public spirited citizens who voluntarily took on the duty, at their own expense, of collecting, maintaining, training and equipping such choruses. It was at the great religious festivals that these plays were produced. For instance, at the city Dionysia there were produced three tragedies, five comedies and five dithyrambs. Men had to be found to provide the choruses for them all. . . . The men who undertook these duties out of their own pocket and out of love for their city were called *chorēgoi*. . . .

The word has a certain lavishness in it. It never means to equip in any cheeseparing and miserly way; it means lavishly to pour out everything that is necessary for a noble performance. *Epichorēgein* went out into a larger world and it grew to mean not only to equip a chorus but to be responsible for any kind of equipment. It can mean to equip an army with all the necessary provisions; it can mean to equip the soul with all the necessary virtues for life (*The Letters of James and Peter*, rev. ed. [Philadelphia: Westminster, 1976], pp. 298–99).

Back to verse 5: "Make every effort to add to your faith" (NIV). In your faith, your initial believing in Christ, you need to come lavishly, zealously, diligently alongside what Christ has done and do everything *you* can possibly do. That's what will continue to yield the fruit of assurance in your life.

What does a believer need to pursue in his or her life to bring about this experience of assurance? In verses 5-7, Peter makes it very plain: excellence, knowledge, self-control, patience, godliness, and love.

Excellence

We begin with "moral excellence." The Greek term *aretē* is also translated "virtue." In classical times it commonly referred to the God-given ability to perform heroic deeds. It came to refer to that quality in a person's life that makes him or her stand out as excellent. It can also refer to an object. A knife was said to be *aretē* if it cut well. A horse was *aretē* if it ran strong and fast. A singer was *aretē* if he or she sang well.

The term never referred to cloistered virtue or virtue in a vacuum. It's not an attitude but an action. Some have suggested that it might mean moral energy. Lexicographers seem to be afraid that someone will think the word has a static meaning when it doesn't. This moral energy gives us the power to perform deeds of excellence.

Let me ask you a simple question: Who is our model for that kind of excellence? Jesus Christ. Paul described the believer's pursuit of excellence as pressing on "toward the goal for the prize of the upward call of God in Christ Jesus" (Phil. 3:14). Spiritual excellence is pursuing Christlikeness. Never give up that pursuit. As Paul said to the Thessalonians, "Excel still more" (1 Thes. 4:1).

Knowledge

Moral excellence cannot occur in a vacuum. At its heart there must be knowledge. The Greek word *gnosis* refers to insight, discernment, and truth properly comprehended. We must first understand how to conduct ourselves properly before we can make any progress in doing so. Moral excellence is dependent on *gnosis*, knowledge of a high character and quality.

It's frightening to realize that our culture has more interest in emotion than knowledge and thinking. That's evident when people more often ask, "How will it make me feel?" instead of

"Is it true?" That wrong focus is also evident in today's theology, where the predominant questions are, "Will it divide?" and "Will it offend?" rather than, "Is it right?" The people of Berea were "noble-minded" because "they received the Word with great eagerness, examining the Scriptures daily" (Acts 17:11). They were interested in finding truth, not good feelings or pleasant circumstances.

In his book, *Right Thinking*, Bill Hull wrote, "What scares me is the anti-intellectual, anti-critical-thinking philosophy that has spilled over into the church. This philosophy tends to romanticize the faith, making the local church into an experience center. . . . Their concept of 'church' is that they are spiritual consumers and that the church's job is to meet their felt needs" ([Colorado Springs: Navpress, 1985], p. 66). Many people are going to church not to think or reason about the truth, but to get a certain feeling.

But living by emotions rather than right thinking will produce instability. John Stott explained why in his book *Your Mind Matters*: "Sin has more dangerous effects on our faculty of feeling than on our faculty of thinking, because our opinions are more easily checked and regulated by revealed truth than our experiences" ([Downers Grove, Ill.: InterVarsity, 1973], p. 16).

Traditional psychiatry sees mankind at the pinnacle of an evolutionary process, yet having many of the same characteristics as less-advanced species. That's why many believe the results of Pavlov's famous stimulus-response experiments with dogs are true for humans as well. However, psychiatrist William Glasser, the father of reality therapy, came to a different conclusion in his book *Stations of the Mind* (New York: Harper & Row, 1981).

In his study of how the brain works, he discovered that people aren't controlled by a predictable stimulus-response factor, but by internal wants and desires. According to Glasser, what people want is predetermined by what influences them—that is, their thinking. Glasser's study shows that human response to outside stimuli is not mechanical, but thoughtful because the mind is the command center determining conduct. It concludes that the critical issue is how people think since that is what influences their actions.

Scripture affirms that conclusion. In Proverbs 23:7, we learn that as a person "thinks within himself, so he is." The Lord says to all people, "Come now, and let us reason together" (Isa. 1:18). Christ told the religious leaders not to look for a sign, but to think about the facts already revealed in Scripture (Matt. 16:1-4; cf. Luke 12:54-57; 16:29-31). And Paul issued a straightforward call for godly thinking (Phil. 4:8). At the heart of it all is the knowledge Peter says to add to our faith (2 Peter 1:5).

Self-control

A building block to that knowledge is the virtue of self-control (2 Peter 1:6). The Greek word used speaks literally of holding oneself in. In Peter's day it was commonly used to describe athletes. The successful ones abstained from sexual indulgence and unhealthy food and drink so they could devote themselves to disciplined exercises for the sake of athletic achievement. You exercise self-control when you control your desires rather than letting your desires control you.

How do you do that? Here are some practical tips that have helped me through the years:

1. *Start small.* Start with your bedroom or office. Clean it, then keep it clean. When something is out of place, train yourself to put it where it belongs. Then extend that discipline of neatness to the rest of your home.

2. *Be on time.* That may not sound very spiritual, but it's important. As Benjamin Franklin said in *Poor Richard's Almanac,* "Dost thou love life? Then do not squander time, for that's the stuff life is made of" (June 1746). That's not just a nice sentiment; it's a scriptural principle (cf. Ecc. 8:6; Eph. 5:15-16). If

you're supposed to be somewhere at a specific time, be there on time. Develop the ability to discipline your desires, activities, and demands so you can arrive on time.

3. *Do the hardest job first.* Doing that will keep the hardest jobs from being left undone.

4. *Organize your life.* Plan—don't just react to circumstances. Use a calendar and make a daily list of things you need to accomplish. If you don't control your time, everything else will.

5. *Accept correction.* Correction helps make you more disciplined because it shows you what you need to avoid. Don't shun criticism; accept it gladly. Now you may not put your hands to your ears, but beware of the more sophisticated ways of shunning criticism. Do you interrupt the person who's criticizing you, flare up in anger, or start pointing out his or her faults? That person is bound to have plenty, being human, but you are speaking out of turn. Give the person a little credit for being brave enough to speak to you when it would be much easier not to. Chances are, he or she has your best interests at heart. Listen patiently and calmly and with a reasonably pleasant expression on your face—don't intimidate by looking away, sighing, or showing other signs of frustration. Do not dare to speak until the person is completely finished, and when you do, thank the person for caring enough to speak to you, apologize if appropriate, and take what was said to heart.

6. *Practice self-denial.* Learn to say no to your feelings, doing what you know to be right even if you don't feel like doing it. Occasionally deny yourself things that are all right just to remind your body who's boss. The next time you want a big hot fudge sundae, order ice tea instead—even if you're skinny! That might sound a little silly, but I've found that cultivating discipline in the physical realm has a way of spilling over into the spiritual.

7. *Welcome responsibility.* When you have an opportunity to do something that needs to be done and you have a talent in that area, volunteer for it. Welcoming responsibility forces you to organize yourself.

At the heart of moral excellence is knowledge or spiritual discernment, and at the heart of that is self-control. False teachers pervert that logical and moral progression. They typically claim that their true and secret knowledge frees them from the need for self-control. But from Peter we learn that any theology that divorces faith from conduct is heresy. Self-control is one of the greatest Christian virtues.

Perseverance

So is perseverance, the godly by-product of self-control. The Greek term used in 2 Peter 1:6, *hupomonē*, refers to endurance in doing what is right and never giving in to temptation or difficulty. Michael Green commented, "The mature Christian does not give up. His Christianity is like the steady burning of a star rather than the ephemeral brilliance (and speedy eclipse) of a meteor" (*The Second General Epistle of Peter and the General Epistle of Jude* [Grand Rapids: Eerdmans, 1968], p. 69).

Lexicographers find *hupomonē* to be a slippery word to pin down. There really is no English equivalent. It isn't a common word in classical Greek, but is frequently used in Scripture of the toils and troubles that come upon a person against his will, making life extremely difficult and painful. It even brings along the thought of death. In the apocryphal books of Maccabees it refers to the spiritual staying power that enabled men and women to die for their faith in God, as they did in the Maccabean Revolution commemorated each year in the Hanukkah celebration.

William Barclay noted that *hupomonē*

is usually translated patience, but patience is too passive a word. Cicero defines *patientia*, its Latin equivalent, as: "The voluntary and daily suffering of hard and difficult things, for the sake of honour and usefulness." Didymus of Alexandria writes on the temper of Job: "It is not that the righteous man must be without feeling, although he must patiently bear the things which afflict him; but it is true virtue when a man deeply feels the things he toils against, but nevertheless despises sorrows for the sake of God."

Hupomonē does not simply accept and endure; there is always a forward look in it. It is said of Jesus . . . that for the joy that was set before him, he endured the Cross, despising the shame (Hebrews 12:2). That is *hupomonē*, Christian steadfastness. It is the courageous acceptance of everything that life can do to us and the transmuting of even the worst event into another step on the upward way (p. 303).

Godliness

At the heart of this persevering endurance is godliness (2 Peter 1:6). In 1 Timothy 6:6, Paul tells us that "godliness with contentment is great gain" (NIV). "Godliness" (Gk., *eusebeia*) is often used in the pastoral epistles. It refers to reverence or piety. I like to think of it as godlikeness. There is great gain in reflecting God's nature and being content with the way things are in your life.

Eusebeia speaks of a practical awareness of God in every area of life—a God consciousness. It used to be translated "true religion." It could be translated "true worship." Josephus, a first-century Jewish historian, contrasted it with the word for idolatry. *Eusebeia* gives God His rightful place by worshiping Him as He ought to be worshiped. Idolatry does the opposite.

I am saddened about the state of worship in North America. As I traveled to different churches during my sabbatical, I saw little of what could biblically be considered true worship. There were lots of rituals, programs, and ministry routines, but not much reverence for God. When I preached messages on the glory of God and true worship, people would say, "We never heard about stuff like that before." That grieved me to the point of writing an entire book on the topic of worship (*The Ultimate Priority* [Chicago: Moody, 1983]).

Now my church isn't immune from this problem. I remember someone expressing the fear that Grace Church, a large church, was becoming too much like a business with all kinds of policies and programs. If we are, God help us. We will end up as dead as the church at Sardis (Rev. 3:1).

The bottom line of worship is that it is more than a formal church activity; it is personal before it is public. The believer is to love and adore God not with stained glass and organ music, but with a life of reverence for God and devotion to His holy will. He or she says with David, "I have set the Lord continually before me" (Ps. 16:8). False teachers are irreverent, irreligious, and ungodly, but true Christians pursue a practical awareness of God in every detail of life. Whatever church you are in, remember to set the Lord before you and worship Him.

Love

In 2 Peter 1:7, godliness leads to the virtues Peter describes as brotherly kindness and love. A love for God leads to a love for others — the two great commandments according to Jesus (Matt. 22:36-40), perhaps because they sum up the Ten Commandments. The Apostle John spoke very plainly about the connection between the two: "If someone says, 'I love God,' and hates his brother, he is a liar; for the one who does not love his brother whom he has seen, cannot love God whom he has not seen" (1 John 4:20). You can't get more practical about Christian love than that!

Nevertheless, you'll always find people spiritualizing love into a meaningless term. Perhaps you've heard someone say, "I love so-and-so in the Lord." Translation: "That person irks me, but he's a believer, so I gotta say I love him!" That's not Christlike love. To love someone in the Lord is to love him or her as Jesus loves that person — genuinely and sacrificially.

I learned a lot about sacrificial love during my sabbatical. My wife and I selected this verse as a theme for our family as we started our trip: "Give preference to one another in honor"

(Rom. 12:10). With four kids in a van for ninety days, it was necessary to live by a verse like that!

Love is so practical. "Brotherly kindness" (2 Peter 1:7) is a translation of the Greek word *philadelphia*. I think the best translation is "friendship." We're to be affectionate toward one another. One of my greatest fears is that people will come to Grace Church and sit on the fringes without developing any relationships. They come just to hear the preacher and listen to the music. Then they go their way. It can be easy to do that in a large church. But we're not to do that—we're to add friendships to our faith, and be continually involved in Christian discipleship.

For some reason, many people believe there is a great mystery surrounding discipleship. Many churches want to know more about discipleship—as if it's some secret program. But discipleship is nothing more than a friendship with a spiritual perspective. The conversation between disciples is about God, not the weather. But discipleship also involves observing how your Christian friends handle the daily affairs of life. Build friendships, join or start a Bible-study fellowship, but don't limit yourself to a small group and keep everyone else out.

When I was in Delaware during my sabbatical, I talked to a pastor who attended one of the annual pastors' conferences we hold at our church. I asked him what stood out in his mind about the conference. He said, "The love of the people for each other. I was drawn to tears when I sensed them worshiping God in the midst of genuine love." "By this all men will know that you are My disciples," Jesus says, "if you have love for one another" (John 13:35).

There are three common Greek words for love. *Eros* is the love that takes. A person who exhibits *eros* loves someone for what he or she can get out of that person. It's the love typical of the world—sexual and lustful with a bent toward self-gratification. *Phileō* is the love of give and take. In other words, I love you because of what I get from you *and* what I can give to you. It's the give and take of friendship.

Agapē is the love that gives. There's no taking involved. It is completely unselfish. It seeks the highest good for another no matter what the cost, demonstrated supremely by Christ's sacrifice on our behalf. That is the kind of love the virtues in 2 Peter 1 lead to.

What does this love look like? A survey of the *one anothers* in the New Testament gives us a good picture. We're to:

- confess our sins to one another (James 5:16).
- forgive one another (Col. 3:13).
- bear one another's burdens (Gal. 6:2).
- rebuke one another (Titus 1:13).
- comfort one another (1 Thes. 4:18).
- encourage one another to do good (Heb. 10:24-25).
- edify one another (Rom. 14:19).
- counsel one another (Rom. 15:14).
- submit to one another (Eph. 5:21).
- instruct one another (Col. 3:16).
- be hospitable to one another (1 Peter 4:9-10).
- bear with one another (Col. 3:12-13).
- pray for one another (James 5:16).
- serve one another (Gal. 5:13).

All those *one anothers* clearly indicate the responsibilities that we as believers have toward one another throughout our lives.

As I look at the life of our Lord Jesus Christ, I see someone who was involved with individuals. He was a caring, sensitive, loving friend who personally interacted in the lives of others. He brought joy to a wedding. He associated with drunkards who needed help to the extent that people falsely started calling Him one too. He met with weak and unimportant people and made them eternally important. He met with perverse and hostile people, revealing a warmth that made Him approachable.

We as a church must be a loving community that shares with one another. So often we think we've done our spiritual duty if we've just gone to church. God help us if that's our perspective of what a church should be! Do your part to enhance the church by being characterized by brotherly kindness and love.

Fruitfulness

If excellence, knowledge, self-control, perseverance, godliness, and love "are yours and are increasing, they render you neither useless nor unfruitful in the true knowledge of our Lord Jesus Christ" (2 Peter 1:8). If you want to enjoy assurance in all its richness, diligently pursue all those virtues. Why? Because they produce a fruitful Christian life, and nothing is more indicative of true salvation than that. Fruitfulness was the criterion Jesus used in distinguishing between the true and the false (Matt. 7:15-20).

The word translated "useless" is used in the discourse on dead faith from James 2. If you add virtue in your life, you won't be dead in terms of your effectiveness.

"Unfruitful" refers to a lack of productivity. It is used in Jude 12 to characterize apostates and false teachers, who are like trees without fruit, and in Matthew 13:22 of the person with a weedy heart. Such a person refuses to let go of his or her worldliness that the seed of God's saving Gospel might truly take root. When you fail to live a virtuous life, you are indistinguishable from an apostate or a worldly hanger-on who leeches off the church.

"In the true knowledge of our Lord Jesus Christ" means that Peter was referring here to true Christians, who possess the true knowledge as opposed to a false knowledge. Because of that great privilege, you as a believer have the capacity to live a virtuous life (cf. 2 Peter 1:3; Eph. 1:3). When you do, you will have assurance.

Beware of Spiritual Amnesia

In 2 Peter 1:9, Peter describes what happens when you don't. "He who lacks these [virtues] is blind or short-sighted, having forgotten his purification from his former sins." The blind believer is nearsighted. He has spiritual myopia. The Greek modifying participle here gives us the word *myopia*. Myopia is a condition of the eye in which parallel rays are focused in front of the retina. Nearsighted people focus right in front of them, but the farther out they look, the worse their vision becomes. Distant things are out of focus.

Believers who are not fruitful go spiritually blind because their perspective is limited. They focus on the earth and the things of the earth—the passing fads and fashions of the day. By the time they try to look to eternity, it is so out of focus for them that they can't perceive it. They are victims of spiritual myopia.

The Greek word translated "purification" is the source of our word *catharsis*—often a reference to a deep internal purging or cleansing. These people have forgotten that they were saved from their old sinful lives because they don't see an increase of spiritual virtue in their lives.

Let me put it to you directly: Where you have an increase of moral virtue, you have evidence of salvation and a basis for assurance. Where you have *no* increase of moral virtue, you have *no* evidence of salvation and *no* basis for assurance. Assurance is directly related to what's going on in your life.

Be warned: A failure to diligently pursue spiritual virtue will produce spiritual amnesia. It will dim your vision of your spiritual condition. You may associate some external activity or experience with the moment of your salvation, but you will not feel assured. Richard Bauckham, writing in the *Word Biblical Commentary*, said, "The 'knowledge of Jesus Christ' [v. 8], received at conversion, came as illumination to those who were blind in their pagan ignorance (2 Cor. 4:4), but Christians who do not carry through the moral implications of this knowledge have effectively become blind to it again" (vol. 50, *Jude, 2 Peter* [Waco, Texas: Word, 1983], p. 189). That kind of forgetfulness leads to a repetition of the old sins.

Grow Spiritually

How do you avoid that fate? Peter answered the question this way: "Therefore, brethren, be all the more diligent to make certain about His calling and choosing you; for as long as you practice these [virtues], you will never stumble" (2 Peter 1:10). That verse sounds a lot like verse 5: Be all the more diligent — apply all diligence. The upshot is to make an even greater effort. To do what? Make certain.

Now you don't need to make God certain about His calling and choosing you — He's very sure about who's elected. He wrote our names in the Lamb's Book of Life before the foundation of the world. God is not the issue here; you are. When you are manifesting the reality of your salvation by bearing fruit, you will never fall from confidence into doubt.

There is nothing worse than to fear hell, thinking you're not really saved. I enjoy life. I love my wife, family, and friends. I thoroughly enjoy the church and the men and women who are a part of the fellowship. I'm a very happy person. But if at any moment I were to have doubts about my salvation, I would not enjoy one day of my life because I would live in fear. Because I have confidence about my future, that frees me to enjoy every day and whatever it brings as a gift from God. You can too.

In simplest terms, the way to be certain about your salvation is to grow spiritually. You'll do that when you "practice," as Peter said, excellence, knowledge, self-control, perseverance, godliness, and love. If you do, you'll never stumble into doubt, despair, depression, grief, or fear over your spiritual condition. You'll always have confidence and full assurance. Your calling and election will be sure in your mind based on what you see in your life.

Enjoy Great Spiritual Reward

Now that's a great blessing, but it is in fact greater than you might think at first glance. Peter elaborates in verse 11: "For in this way the entrance into the eternal kingdom of our Lord and

Savior Jesus Christ will be abundantly supplied to you." That verse requires careful thought.

Peter was saying by pursuing virtue, you'll not only enjoy assurance here, but also receive eternal reward in the life to come, which is the goal of our spiritual pilgrimage. Some people would lead you to believe you can come to Jesus Christ and believe in Him at a moment in time, and then live any way you want. Some people might even say it's nice if you decide to pursue moral virtue, but if you don't, you'll still get into the kingdom just the same. Not really.

If you're truly a Christian, but do not diligently pursue moral virtue, you will live in doubt and despair, perpetually worrying about your spiritual condition and wondering whether you're really saved because you're not seeing increased holiness in your life. In the future you will enter the kingdom, but you'll find you won't receive an abundant supply of reward on that day. You will receive praise from God, but it won't be to the degree that it could have been had you pursued moral excellence and the like.

A Jewish teenager named Marvin helped run his family's luncheonette in a Jewish neighborhood in Philadelphia. He came to believe in Christ as the promised Messiah and suffered frequent persecution as a result. Thinking it was all too much, he enlisted with the Marines when he turned eighteen to escape the peer pressure and ridicule. The lady who led him to the Lord said this to him before he left: "You're a true Christian, Marvin. . . . One day when your earthly life ends you will go to Heaven because of what the Messiah has done for you. But if, when you get to Heaven, there is a great big parade and if, in the front of the parade there is a great big band—if you don't change your way of living, you'll be so far back in the line that you won't even hear the music" (Marvin J. Rosenthal, *Jewish and Twice Born: A Testimonial* [Orlando, Fla.: Zion's Hope, n.d.], pp. 10–11). Marvin got the message and in time devoted his life to reaching his people with the truth of the Messiah. He didn't want to miss receiving an abundant supply of reward on that day (2 Peter 1:11).

It is a basic Christian truth that we are to live our lives in light of eternity—to lay up treasures in heaven, to pursue the virtuous things of gold, silver, and precious stones, and not the lesser things of wood, hay, and stubble. Those who have diligently and faithfully pursued holiness will receive a superabundant reward. And lest you fear that's a crass motive for doing good, remember that believers will cast their rewards or crowns before the throne of God as an act of homage (cf. Rev. 4:10; 2 Tim. 4:7-8).

All Christians bear some fruit, but there's obviously a choice involved. Some Christians choose to make a minor effort at spiritual virtue, while others make a major effort at it. While God "richly supplies us with all things to enjoy" (1 Tim. 6:17), with "the riches of the glory of His inheritance" (Eph. 1:18), and with "the surpassing riches of His grace in kindness toward us in Christ Jesus" (2:7), Peter points out the balancing truth that there are degrees of reward God gives to us based on our diligent pursuit of righteousness. Stated more plainly, abundant sowing means abundant reaping. Rewards of grace in eternity correspond to the work of grace in time.

At salvation, the matter of entrance into the kingdom was settled, but not the manner of entrance.

Look at your life. If you don't see moral virtue, you don't have any evidence to verify your salvation. If you do—though obviously not in perfection, but it's there and increasing—you have reason to be "certain about [God's] calling and choosing you" (2 Peter 1:10).

Delight in the Blessings of Assurance

Let's make this very practical by considering the blessings of such assurance:

It makes you love and praise God. If you know you're saved, you will praise God for that. If you don't, how can you be filled with loving praise and gratitude?

It adds joy to all your earthly duties and trials. If you know you're saved, no matter what comes up, you are assured that all will work out well for you in the end. Any difficulty is easier to handle when you know it's temporary.

It makes you zealous in obedience and service. Doubt breeds apathy; assurance breeds industry. Doubt discourages service; assurance encourages it.

It gives you victory in temptation. If you know you belong to God, you can be assured that "no temptation has overtaken you but such as is common to man; and God is faithful, who will not allow you to be tempted beyond what you are able; but with the temptation will provide the way of escape also, that you may be able to endure it" (1 Cor. 10:13). How wonderful to know you can overcome whatever temptation comes your way—no matter how strong it is! If you should stumble, however, you also have the assurance that it cannot change your eternal destiny. On the other hand, if you're not assured of your salvation, the temptations you face will discourage and depress you. You'll wonder whether you'll be able to deal with them or whether they might damn you to hell if you fall victim to one or two of them.

It makes you content, even if you have little in this world. If you are assured of your salvation, you know you have a rich heavenly inheritance to look forward to, but in the meantime you also know that God "shall supply all your needs according to His riches in glory in Christ Jesus" (Phil. 4:19). But if you're not sure you're saved and fear this life might be all you have to live for, you'll grasp for everything this world has to offer. And when things don't go as you plan, you'll feel cheated.

It removes the fear of death. If you know you're a Christian, you can face death in full confidence that, right as you leave this life, you'll enter into the very presence of Jesus Christ. If you don't, however, you'll be scared to die—exponentially more than someone who hasn't heard about Christ because you've been made aware of the terrors of hell.

God says you can make your calling and election absolutely

sure. You never need to stumble into doubt and despair. All you have to do is diligently pursue excellence, knowledge, self-control, perseverance, godliness, and love. As a result, you'll enjoy all the benefits of assurance and realize a rich heavenly reward to the glory of God.

EIGHT

Gaining Victory

We've been blessed in our church over the last months and years to have welcomed many new Christians into the fellowship. That prompted me to take the congregation through a topical series on the Book of Romans regarding salvation and the believer's relationship to Christ. My goal was to provide a solid biblical foundation for those new to the family of faith—and a refreshing reminder to vintage Christians. I would like to share with you one of the highlights of that study.

These verses from Romans 8 have given me great assurance through the years: "Brethren, we are under obligation, not to the flesh, to live according to the flesh—for if you are living according to the flesh, you must die; but if by the Spirit you are putting to death the deeds of the body, you will live" (vv. 12-13). The key phrase is "by the Spirit," often translated "through the Spirit." It is our means to spiritual progress and victory, and nothing provides greater assurance than seeing results.

First the Bad News
We as Christians are often in need of such encouragement because we are all engaged in a major struggle with ourselves.

That was the point Paul made in Romans 7, using himself as an example. This is some of what he went through in his inner battle:

> That which I am doing, I do not understand; for I am not practicing what I would like to do, but I am doing the very thing I hate. . . . The good that I wish, I do not do; but I practice the very evil that I do not wish. . . . I find then the principle that evil is present in me, the one who wishes to do good . . . waging war against the law of my mind, and making me a prisoner of the law of sin which is in my members. . . . Wretched man that I am! (vv. 15, 19, 21, 23-24)

What's going on here? As believers, we have been made new in Christ. His righteousness is not only imputed to us judicially, but also granted to us in reality by the indwelling presence of the Holy Spirit. We possess new life. We have become partakers of the very life of God. We now have holy longings, desiring what is righteous, godly, virtuous, pure, and lovely. All that wells up within us and then collides head-on with our unre-deemed human flesh — the part of us that retains our connection to this fallen, imperfect world. That conflict makes for an ongo-ing and frankly exasperating struggle at times.

Have you noticed a pattern of bad news then good news in understanding God's revealed truth? You can't accept the good news of salvation until you deal with the bad news of sin. Likewise, you can't experience victory in Christ until you deal with the residual sin in your life. As we've been noting all along, some believers become so confused by the bad news of the internal struggle that's part of being a Christian, they doubt their salvation altogether. They need to see the good news: We *can* win the struggle!

In Romans 8, Paul tells us that we overcome the debilitating power of the remaining flesh "through the Spirit." There's no victory over the flesh apart from the Holy Spirit. The flesh has no power over itself. The leopard cannot change its spots. If there's going to be any conquering of the flesh, it's going to be through something other than the flesh, namely, the Spirit of God working in us.

The question the thoughtful Christian needs to be asking himself or herself is, *How do I let the Spirit of God take control so I can experience victory in my spiritual life?* In verses 12-13, that question is answered by unfolding the pattern for victory. The text begins by providing a very basic understanding.

No Victim Mentality

In verse 12, Paul states, "We are under obligation, not to the flesh, to live according to the flesh." Know that you aren't under any obligation to live after the flesh. Stated most plainly, you don't *have* to sin. There's nothing within you that is so compelling and dominating and powerful and sovereign that you just can't help but sin. "No temptation has overtaken you but such as is common to man," Paul tells the Corinthians, "and God is faithful, who will not allow you to be tempted beyond what you are able, but with the temptation *will provide the way of escape* also, that you may be able to endure it" (1 Cor. 10:13, emphasis added). There's always a way to avoid giving in to sin.

Before becoming a Christian, you lived according to the flesh as a way of life. You were motivated, guided, and dominated by the complex of sinful desires that make up the flesh. But you're not anymore. Paul explained the change that took place in this way: "Those who are according to the flesh set their minds on the things of the flesh. . . . The mind set on the flesh is death . . . because the mind set on the flesh is hostile toward God; for it does not subject itself to the Law of God, for it is not even able to do so; and those who are in the flesh cannot please God" (Rom. 8:5-8). That's Paul's definition of an unbeliever, but then he says this: "However you are not in the flesh" (v. 9). You're not there anymore. It is simply a statement of fact.

Now you have a context for Paul's declaration in verse 12, loosely paraphrased, "You're certainly not under obligation to live like that anymore, are you?" How ridiculous! How totally contradictory for "brethren," as he called us, who have the privileges of justification and sanctification—being freed from sin and death and the mastery of the flesh—to think we're under some kind of obligation to do what is wrong.

If you sin, it isn't God's fault; it's your fault—it's your choice. In a sense, it isn't even sin's fault because as a believer, you're not under any obligation to do what it says.

That's a very important concept to grasp because it keeps you from seeing yourself as a victim. You'll never realize spiritual victory in your life as long as you think you are being overpowered by something you have no control over. I don't care whether it's alcohol, drugs, or sexual perversion—you don't have to give in. You owe nothing to the flesh, nothing at all.

Sure there will be lapses into fleshly behavior. In 1 Corinthians 3, Paul does talk about that, but the point Paul was making there is that a Christian acting carnally or fleshly is acting like an unbeliever. Sure Paul said, "I haven't made it, I haven't arrived, I'm not what I ought to be, but I'm pressing toward the mark" (Phil. 3, author's paraphrase). I don't have to convince you that you're not perfect. But what's essential to understand is that when you sin, it's because you choose not to follow God's way of escape. You do not have an unconquerable enemy. Let that make an indelible impression on you because you'll never get victory over sin if you believe sin is an unbeatable foe.

Victory is available to you by virtue of a positive reality: the indwelling Spirit, and a negative reality: the fact that you don't have any compelling obligation to live the way you used to live, or go the way of the world.

There's also a positive to that negative: Yes, you're not under obligation to commit sin, but you are under obligation to do what's right. In Romans 8:13, Paul puts it in this way: "If you are living according to the flesh, you must die; but if by the Spirit you are putting to death the deeds of the body, you will live." Those are axiomatic statements—self-evident truths that need no proof. The unbeliever is headed for eternal death, the believer to life eternal.

Note how Paul defined his terms. The unbeliever is one who lives according to the flesh. The believer is one who, by the Spirit, puts to death the deeds of the body. If you're a person who is killing the deeds of the body in the power of the Spirit, that's evidence of your salvation. If you're spiritually bent, you're headed for heaven.

Living according to the flesh would be foolish because that's the way unbelievers live, and you're not one of them anymore. You have a new bent, a new direction, characterized by killing the deeds of your flesh through the power of the Spirit. If you're a Christian, that will be true of you—but it needs to be more and more true of you.

Kill the Enemy

Let's face it: All of us could be killing more of our personal sins than we are. The crucial question to ask yourself is, *How do I kill sin in my life?* Here are some practical steps for establishing a pattern of victory in your life and experiencing the assurance that results from following those steps.

Don't Sugarcoat Sin in Your Life.

Rather, recognize the presence of sin in your flesh. I believe the most common reason sin defeats Christians is that a particular sin has so totally deceived them, they don't honestly evaluate its reality. They're not dealing with the issue. It's easy to justify your sin as a quirk of your personality or a product of your environment. If you sugarcoat your habitual sins as idiosyncrasies, prenatal predilections, or whatever other excuses are currently popular, you won't see them for what they are.

The first step to victory in warfare is identifying the enemy. If you don't know what to shoot at, how are you going to hit it? How can you eliminate from your life what you don't even identify as needing to be eliminated? Sin is not only wicked; it is deceitful. And it's there, believe me, it's there.

Perhaps it's no great shock to you that sin is present in your life. Realize, however, that it likes to hide. It likes to make itself at home in you so it doesn't appear at all out of the ordinary.

David knew that, which is why he prayed, "Who can understand his errors? Cleanse Thou me from secret faults. Keep back Thy servant also from presumptuous sins" (Ps. 19:12-13, KJV). Sin necessitates an internal search-and-destroy mission. That's what we see going on in David's heart when he said, "Search me, O God, and know my heart; try me, and know my thoughts; and see if there be any wicked way in me" (139:23-24, KJV).

What's so fallacious about most contemporary psychotherapy is that instead of making you deal with the reality of your present spiritual condition, it drags you into the past and blames someone else for your problems. You must deal with whatever sins you find debilitating your life. Look for them to manifest themselves in anger and bitter words, unkind thoughts, excessive criticism, self-conceit, lack of understanding, impatience, weak prayers, immoral thoughts, and even overt sins.

Two times the Prophet Haggai says, "Consider your ways!" (Hag. 1:5, 7) Take a good look at yourself. The writer of 1 Kings 8:38 says to know the plague in your own heart. Begin by examining your own life to see what's really there.

Be Consistent in Dealing with Sin.
That is the second step to gaining victory in your spiritual life. "My heart is fixed, O God," says the psalmist, "my heart is fixed" (Ps. 57:7, KJV). That speaks of undivided devotion to God in every area of life. If you have that kind of attitude, you won't be satisfied with cleaning up sin in one area of your life, but leaving it alone in another. The seasoned Christian knows that if sin lives anywhere, it will crawl everywhere. It is the most

noxious and fastest-growing weed in existence.

Another psalmist wrote, "Then I shall not be ashamed when I look upon all Thy commandments" (119:6). He knew his life wouldn't be right until he showed the proper respect to every command of God. Don't make allowances for any sins in your life. Take each one seriously as it comes to light, and deal with it biblically.

Use the Word to Poison Your Sins.

The way to kill sin in your life is to feed it Scripture. It's a foolproof poison against the weed of sin. Here's why: As we noted in the previous chapter, whatever dominates your thinking will dominate your behavior. If you feed yourself a steady diet of God's glorious truth, meditating upon each morsel received, that will inevitably produce a godly life.

Our passage in Romans 8 tells us that as we live by the Spirit, we put to death the sin in our lives (v. 13). A related passage says this: "Do not get drunk with wine, for that is dissipation, but be filled with the Spirit" (Eph. 5:18). A passage parallel to that one equates being filled with the Spirit with letting the Word of God dwell richly within you (Col. 3:16). Victorious, spirit-filled living requires that you give yourself to the Word. Saturate yourself in it. Hear it preached and taught. Learn it yourself and meditate on it day and night. That's what preceded Joshua's great victories (Josh. 1:8), and it is the necessary precursor to yours as well.

Use Prayer to Expose Your Hidden Sins.

Ask God to help you be honest with Him. Begin praying, "Lord, I want You to reveal my sin. I want You to blow away the dust that's covering it. I want You to show it to me just the way it is." That's an important part of communing with God, and is the heart of true confession. You can confess a few sins here and there, but until you pray, "God, show me all the sins of my life, and may they become as detestable to me as they are to You that I might never repeat them," your prayers will be lacking a spirit of repentance.

A way I test my heart in prayer is, if after saying, "Lord, please forgive me for that sin," I am wholly willing to add this P.S.: "And Lord, may I never do it again." That keeps me honest before God. I would feel like a hypocrite asking forgiveness for something I fully intend to repeat. Honest prayers are a preservative against sin. They expose secret sins and weaken prevailing sins. Through prayer you'll derive strength in your fellowship with the Holy God to kill the sins in your life.

Relentlessly Move Forward.

Once you leave that private place where you've fixed your gaze on God, meditated on the Word, and communed with God in prayer over your sin, step out into the public arena on a course of obedience. Paul said, "Not that I have already obtained it, or have already become perfect, but I press on" (Phil. 3:12). He hadn't reached the heavenly goal of Christlikeness (v. 14), but he was headed in the right direction by doing right.

A good description of the Christian life is, as Peter said, "obedience to the truth" (1 Peter 1:22). If you want to engage in a real battle with sin, just set your course day by day, moment by moment, and step by step on a path of obedience to God's Word. At first it will seem hard and progress will seem slow, but if you stay with it, obedience will become habitual. Simply stay on the path that God has laid out in His Word. By doing so you'll be training yourself toward godliness.

Do a Personal Inventory.

Start the training process by considering a few basic questions:

1. *How is your zeal for the things of God?* Is your heart cold toward God? Has sin made you indifferent to times of communion with Him? Do you have little or no interest in His presence or in how His Word is regarded by others? Can you relate at all to the psalmist's saying, "My eyes shed streams of water,

because they do not keep Thy law"? (Ps. 119:136) Do you earnestly contend for the faith and uphold the truth? Do you delight in worship, or do you say with the unfaithful Jews of Malachi's day, "My, how tiresome it is!" (Mal. 1:13) Do you enjoy singing praises to God?

2. *Do you love the Word?* Do you find yourself drawn to the Word? Do you have a strong desire to find out what it means — even in the difficult areas?

3. *How do you regard prayer?* Do you see it for the privilege that it truly is? Are you eager not only to confess your sins before God and experience forgiveness, but also to undergo rigorous self-examination? Do you honestly seek for the Holy Spirit to expose every dirty thing in your life that it might be eliminated?

4. *How do you regard sin in general?* Are you sensitive to sin in the church and in the world? Does it tear at your heart whenever you see sin around you?

Spiritual victory is not an elusive goal. Recognize that as a believer, you're not under any obligation to sin. The Spirit of God has already bent you toward life and given you the means to kill the residual sin in your life. Tap into those means so that you might have a life of virtue, joy, peace, and usefulness to God. If you deal confidently and consistently with the sin in your life, you will experience the effect of righteousness, which Isaiah 32:17 defines as everlasting assurance and security.

NINE

Persevering through It All

A man who had been deeply moved by the death of a friend spoke to the minister who conducted the grave side service. The man expressed his desire to become a Christian, but added, "There's just one thing that makes me hesitate: I'm afraid I won't be able to hold out. I work with a pretty tough group. They're hardly what you would call religious. I don't think there's a real Christian in the bunch, and I know they won't take kindly to there being one."

The minister stooped down to pick up one of the flowers adorning the grave and commented, "Take a good look at this flower. It grew right in the mud and slime and decay of the earth, yet see how clean and spotless it is. That's because God kept it. And He can keep you too!"

You and I will go through our share of slime in this world. Yet one of the greatest comforts God gives to His children is that we will come out smelling like a rose. The theological label for that encouraging reality is *the perseverance of the saints.*

The Happiness Endurance Brings
Awhile back when preaching through the Book of James, I became enthralled with that doctrine when I came to this verse

in my study: "Blessed is a man who perseveres under trial; for once he has been approved, he will receive the crown of life, which the Lord has promised to those who love Him" (1:12). James later reiterates the same thought: "Behold, we count those blessed who endured" (5:11). People who successfully endure trials are truly happy. One of the main reasons is the sense of assurance that endurance or perseverance brings to the faithful.

James was not saying happiness comes in freedom from trials, but in victory over them—a point similar to the one Paul made regarding victory over sin in our last chapter. There is a big difference. This is not the shallow joy of the spectator who never experienced conflict, but the exuberance of the participant who fought and won.

James was not referring to temptation. If that were the case, he would have said happy is the man who resists it, not happy is the man who endures it. The three key ideas in verse 12 are endurance, trials, and being tested. The same ideas appear in James 1:2-3: "Consider it all joy, my brethren, when you encounter various trials; knowing that the testing of your faith produces endurance." Endurance is the theme of verses 2-12.

Endurance is patiently and triumphantly persevering through difficulty. It connotes passive or even painful survival, and focuses on the outcome of being victorious. The person who goes through trials and comes out a winner never gives up his or her faith or abandons God. That person is revealed to be genuine, and all genuine Christians will receive the crown of life.

Perseverance as Proof

Some people come to church, profess Christ, and even get baptized. Yet when trouble comes into their lives, they're gone. And they may never come back. Maybe they encountered a broken relationship, the death of a loved one, or some other struggle, and the circumstances seemed so overpowering to them that they blamed God and walked away, convinced that Christianity doesn't work.

Persevering through trials is proof of living faith. James identified those who persevere as people who love God (v. 12). That's because loving God is the natural outflow of salvation. John said, "We love [God], because He first loved us" (1 John 4:19). Christianity is a love relationship between God and His children. Salvation is not a transaction whereby God grants us eternal life no matter what our attitude toward Him is. Those who are truly saved have a deep, ongoing love for God.

Earlier John explained, "If anyone loves the world, the love of the Father is not in him" (1 John 2:15). People will love either God or the world, but not both. Unbelievers who profess Christ demonstrate that they love the world when they depart from the truth. It's in a trial that true love is made manifest. "They went out from us," John says, "but they were not really of us; for if they had been of us, they would have remained with us; but they went out, in order that it might be shown that they all are not of us" (1 John 2:19). If you truly love God and His people, you will stick with them through thick and thin.

The Apostle Peter said you'll have reason to rejoice if you do that: "In this you greatly rejoice, even though now for a little while, if necessary, you have been distressed by various trials, that the proof of your faith, being more precious than gold which is perishable, even though tested by fire, may be found to result in praise and glory and honor at the revelation of Jesus Christ; and though you have not seen Him, you love Him, and though you do not see Him now, but believe in Him, you greatly rejoice with joy inexpressible and full of glory" (1 Peter 1:6-8). Your faith is being tested to whatever degree is necessary to prove its genuineness, so you'll be able to stand before the Lord when He returns.

A Christian is so much more than someone who simply at one point in time believed the truth. A true believer has an ongoing love for God that holds fast even in trials. And as we've noted previously, love for God manifests itself through obedience to His Word (1 John 2:5-6; 5:1-3).

As believers, we may experience times of struggle and doubt, but our faith will never be destroyed. We cling to the Lord despite our trials because we love Him. That kind of loving perseverance results in true blessing.

One purpose of testing is to expose the quality of our faith. The phrase in James 1:12 "for when he is tried" (KJV) can be translated "when he is approved after testing." When tests come into your life in the form of loneliness, a death, or a financial loss, God is putting you through the fire, as it were, that you might come out with the dross burned off and your true faith shining bright. Those who hold fast to their trust in God through trials show that their faith is living.

The perseverance of the saints is a major tenant of Reformed Protestant theology. That, as I pointed out in the introduction to this book, is in contrast to teaching that denies believers can ever be sure of their salvation in this life. The Bible teaches that the saints will never abandon their faith—that they will always persevere in believing God through every trial until they are glorified. True believers won't believe for a little while and then bail out.

God at Work on Our Behalf

The Trinity secures us forever so that no Christian who believes in the Lord will ever be lost. Scripture bases the eternal security of the believer on the promise and power of God, the prayers of Christ, and the presence of the Holy Spirit. As you may recall, that was the theme of this book's first chapter. Now in this closing chapter, I'd like to build on that theme. Here are verses throughout Scripture for you to reflect on whenever you're tempted to doubt God's willingness or ability to preserve His people from apostasy and bring them all—including you—to heaven:

• *Psalm 31:24*—"Be of good courage, and [God] shall strengthen your heart, all ye that hope in the Lord" (KJV).

• *Psalm 37:23, 28*—"The steps of a man are established by

the Lord. . . . For the Lord loves justice, and does not forsake His godly ones; they are preserved forever."

• *Psalm 97:10*—"Ye that love the Lord, hate evil: He preserveth the souls of His saints; He delivereth them out of the hand of the wicked" (KJV).

• *Psalm 121:4-7*—"Behold, He who keeps Israel will neither slumber nor sleep. The Lord is your keeper; the Lord is your shade on your right hand. The sun will not smite you by day, nor the moon by night. The Lord will protect you from all evil; He will keep your soul."

• *Luke 22:31-32*—Jesus told Peter, "Satan has demanded permission to sift you like wheat; but I have prayed for you, that your faith may not fail; and you, when once you have turned again, strengthen your brothers." Soon after Jesus said that, Peter committed the very serious sin of denying his association with Christ three times in a row. But later he repented and was restored to Christ and to useful service, just as our Lord had prayed.

• *John 6:37, 39*—Jesus said, "All that the Father gives Me shall come to Me. . . . And this is the will of Him who sent Me, that of all that He has given Me I lose nothing, but raise it up on the last day." God's will *will* be done. After all, "the gifts and the calling of God are irrevocable" (Rom. 11:29). Jesus later said, "I give eternal life to them [those who follow Him]; and they shall never perish, and no one shall snatch them out of My hand. My Father, who has given them to Me, is greater than all; and no one is able to snatch them out of the Father's hand" (John 10:28-29). It is God who provides salvation and God who will preserve it. No one can undo that—not even you.

• *John 17:20-24*—Jesus prayed for His present and future disciples to enter into the fullness of salvation, and that is a prayer God is certain to answer.

• *Romans 16:25-26*—Paul offered praise to Him who is able to use the Scriptures to establish us in obedience to the faith.

• *Ephesians 1:13-14*—We have been "sealed with that Holy

Spirit of promise, which is the earnest of our inheritance until
the redemption of the purchased possession" (KJV).

• *Philippians 1:6*—"He who began a good work in you will
carry it on to completion until the day of Christ Jesus" (NIV).
Can there be any more encouraging reminder for the struggling
Christian than that? Therefore, be assured of your salvation no
matter how incomplete or imperfect you are right now.

• *1 Thessalonians 5:23-24*—Paul said, "Now may the God of
peace Himself sanctify you entirely; and may your spirit and soul
and body be preserved complete, without blame at the coming
of our Lord Jesus Christ. Faithful is He who calls you, and He
also will bring it to pass." Paul was echoing more than just a
sentiment, but a reality as true as God is true.

• *2 Timothy 1:12*—Paul said, "I know whom I have believed,
and am persuaded that He is able to keep that which I have
committed unto Him against that day" (KJV). Paul committed all
that he was and did to God. That gave him great confidence, for
one of the last things he ever wrote was, "The Lord will deliver
me from every evil deed, and will bring me safely to His heavenly kingdom" (2 Tim. 4:18).

• *1 Peter 1:5*—Peter stated definitively that Christians "are
kept by the power of God" (KJV).

• *1 John 2:1-2*—John said, "If anyone sins, we have an Advocate with the Father, Jesus Christ the righteous; and He Himself
is the propitiation for our sins." Christ constantly intercedes on
our behalf as our Redeemer and Advocate so that any sin we
commit will not alter the status of our salvation.

• *Jude 1*—Jude majestically described believers as "the called,
beloved in God the Father, and kept for Jesus Christ" or "preserved in Jesus Christ." He concluded his brief epistle on that
same grand note: "Now to Him who is able to keep you from
stumbling, and to make you stand in the presence of His glory
blameless with great joy" (v. 24).

The panorama of Scripture overwhelmingly makes the case
for full assurance.

The Human Equation

I grew up hearing the phrases "eternal security" and "once saved, always saved." Now those are accurate descriptions of what Scripture teaches. The Bible doesn't say, "Once saved, but you never know how long." However, some people wrongfully conclude that means you can do anything you want if you're saved—as if God were stuck with you. They emphasize the sovereignty of God and His unchanging promise in securing our salvation, but to the exclusion of how a person who has been spiritually reborn is responsible to live.

The perseverance of the saints is the human response to the predestinating work of God. You reveal you are kept by God if you don't abandon your faith in the midst of a trial.

The paradox of the sovereign work of God and the responsibility of believers is common in Scripture. Believers are saved because God chose them before creation (Eph. 1:4), yet they are not saved without exercising faith (Rom. 10:9-10). They are secure because of the covenant faithfulness of God, but they are still responsible to persevere.

Eternal security is wrought through the power of the Spirit in energizing the true believer to endure all trials. Theologian Louis Berkhof described perseverance as "that continuous operation of the Holy Spirit in the believer, by which the work of divine grace that is begun in the heart, is continued and brought to completion" ([Systematic Theology [Grand Rapids: Eerdmans, 1941], p. 546). So our part is to endure.

Having that theological understanding explains a lot of verses that might otherwise lead the uninformed believer to doubt the security of his or her salvation. Jesus, speaking to His disciples, said, "It is the one who has endured to the end who will be saved" (Matt. 10:22; cf. 24:13). Now at first glance that appears to contradict the truth that God is going to keep us saved, but it doesn't. We are energized to endure by the indwelling Spirit. The mark of true justification is perseverance in righteousness to the very end.

Continuance in the faith is an ongoing theme in the New Testament. Jesus said repeatedly to those "who had believed Him, 'If you abide in My word, then you are truly disciples of Mine' " (John 8:31). Paul adds, "I make known to you, brethren, the gospel which I preached to you, which also you received, in which also you stand, by which also you are saved, if you hold fast the word which I preached to you, unless you believed in vain" (1 Cor. 15:1-2). If you don't hold on to your faith, you show it wasn't real.

Paul spoke further of that principle in his letter to the Colossians: "Although you were formerly alienated and hostile in mind, engaged in evil deeds, yet He has now reconciled you in His fleshly body through death, in order to present you before Him holy and blameless and beyond reproach—*if indeed you continue in the faith* firmly established and steadfast, and not moved away from the hope of the gospel" (1:21-23, emphasis added). You're secure only if you endure, but as a true believer you *will* endure because you are secure. Endurance is the process by which the security of your salvation is verified.

Only the faithful are of the faith. That was the main point the author of Hebrews tried to drive home to his churchgoing audience: "We must pay much closer attention to what we have heard, lest we drift away from it" (2:1). "We have become partakers of Christ, if we hold fast the beginning of our assurance firm until the end" (3:14). "Let us hold fast our confession" (4:14). "We desire that each one of you show the same diligence so as to realize the full assurance of hope until the end, that you may not be sluggish, but imitators of those who through faith and patience inherit the promises" (6:11-12). "We are not of those who shrink back to destruction, but of those who have faith to the preserving of the soul" (10:39).

When a professing believer doesn't endure, he or she has failed the test of genuine faith (1 John 2:19). No trial is so great that it could sever you from your Lord if your faith is genuine (Rom. 8:38-39). Eternal security is a great scriptural truth, but it should never be presented as merely a matter of being once saved, always saved—with no regard for what you believe or do. The writer of Hebrews 12:14 states frankly that only those who continue living holy lives will enter the Lord's presence.

The contemporary trend labeled "easy believism" holds that a one-time decision to accept Christ as Savior—but not necessarily as Lord—is all that it takes to be a Christian. However, the testimony of Scripture is that bare assent to the Gospel facts, divorced from a transforming commitment to Christ for life, is something less than saving faith. (I explored that issue further in my book *The Gospel According to Jesus* [Grand Rapids: Zondervan, 1988].) If a person fails to love and obey the Lord through the trials of life, then there is no evidence that he or she is a true believer. How many people do you know who followed Christ for a while, had some trouble in their lives, and then went away from Him? (cf. John 6:66) Although they may have made a profession of faith in Christ, they cannot be identified as those who love Him because their lives are not characterized by an enduring obedience.

In contrast, all true believers will persevere. The authors of the Westminster Confession of Faith crafted a masterful explanation of that reassuring biblical truth:

They whom God hath accepted in His Beloved, effectually called and sanctified by His Spirit, can neither totally nor finally fall away from the state of grace; but shall certainly persevere therein to the end and be eternally saved. This perseverance of the saints depends, not upon their own free-will, but on the immutability of the decree of election, flowing from the free and unchangeable love of God the Father; upon the efficacy of the merit and intercession of Jesus Christ; the abiding of the Spirit and of the seed of God within them; and the nature of the covenant of grace: from all which ariseth also the certainty and infallibility thereof. Nevertheless they may, through the temptations of

Satan and of the world, the prevalency of corruption remaining in them, and the neglect of the means of their
preservation, fall into grievous sins; and for a time continue therein: whereby they incur God's displeasure, and
grieve His Holy Spirit; come to be deprived of some measure of their graces and comforts; have their hearts hardened, their consciences wounded; hurt and scandalize others, and bring temporal judgments upon themselves (*The
Creeds of Christendom*, vol. 3, Philip Schaff, ed. [Grand
Rapids: Baker, 1977], pp. 636–37).

Christians may get themselves into trouble, but they will never ultimately jettison their faith because God has enabled them
to persevere. Whenever trials come into your life, look at them
as opportunities to persevere and thereby prove the genuineness
of your faith. And having persevered, you can look back and say,
"Yes, I know I belong to the Lord." Look at life that way, and
you won't have any trouble being assured of your salvation.

Perhaps you're wondering—especially if you're a new believer—whether it's *only* in looking back on a life of faithfulness
that you can have an absolute sense of assurance and security.
What about now in the thick of life? Rest easy: Our Heavenly
Father wants His children to be assured of their eternal security
throughout their pilgrimage on earth.

What you need to do is trust in His promise to sovereignly
preserve you. Just as you exercised faith in God's saving work
when you first came to Christ, you now need to exercise faith in
His preserving work. Look again at the Scriptures I listed high-
lighting God's work on our behalf. Commit several of them to
memory, especially Philippians 1:6 and Jude 24. If you have
made the proper commitment to Christ, you can be assured that
the Holy Spirit will enable you to persevere. Thus you can say
with Paul, "*I know* whom I have believed and *I am convinced*
that He is able to guard what I have entrusted to Him until that
day" (2 Tim. 1:12, emphasis added).

The Crown at the End

The reward for the believer who does not collapse under trials is eternal life. James said, "Once he has been approved, he will receive the crown of life" (1:12). The "crown of life" is an appositional genitive in the Greek text, which means it could literally be translated, "the crown that is life." The crown is eternal life, which God has promised to those who love Him. It is the believer's ultimate reward.

Paul, Peter, and John wrote of the same great reality. Paul knew he would soon be killed. What comforted him in his last days was knowing this: "In the future there is laid up for me the crown of righteousness, which the Lord, the righteous Judge, will award to me on that day; and not only to me, but also to all who have loved His appearing" (2 Tim. 4:8). When Christ returns for His church, all believers will be granted a life of eternal righteousness in both body and soul.

Peter wrote, "When the Chief Shepherd appears, you will receive the unfading crown of glory" (1 Peter 5:4). And John recorded this promise from the lips of Christ to the persevering church: "Be faithful until death, and I will give you the crown of life" (Rev. 2:10). We who persevere will receive this crown.

Now I want you to keep in mind an important distinction. Endurance does not earn eternal life, but it is the proof of true faith and love, and that is rewarded by eternal life.

In the world of ancient Greece, the word translated "crown" (stephanos) often referred to the wreath put around the head of a victor in an athletic event, such as the original Olympic games. In the spiritual arena, the Lord will reward with eternal life those who demonstrate with the perseverance of a victorious athlete that they were truly saved.

Perhaps the course laid out before you is rough. Maybe, like the man I spoke of at the beginning of this chapter, you're afraid you won't be able to hold out. As the minister assured him, let me assure you: You *will* hold out if you're God's child. He will see to that for sure.

I have written like this to you
who already believe in the name of God's Son
so that you may be quite sure that,
here and now, you possess eternal life.

1 John 5:13 (PH)

The work of righteousness will be peace,
and the effect of righteousness,
quietness and assurance forever.

Isaiah 32:17 (NKJV)

Personal and Group Study Guide

Before beginning your personal or group study of *Saved Without a Doubt*, take time to read these introductory comments.

If you are working through the study on your own, you may want to adapt certain sections (for example, the icebreakers), and record your responses to all questions in a separate notebook. You might find it more enriching or motivating to study with a partner with whom you can share answers or insights.

If you are leading a group, you may want to ask your group members to read each assigned chapter and work through the study questions before the group meets. This isn't always easy for busy adults, so encourage them with occasional phone calls or notes between meetings. Help members manage their time by pointing out how they can cover a few pages each day. Also have them identify a regular time of the day or week that they can devote to the study. They too may write their responses to the questions in notebooks.

Notice that each session includes the following features:

Chapter Theme—a brief statement summarizing the chapter.
Icebreaker—an activity to help group members get better acquainted with the session topic and/or with each other.
Group Discovery Questions—a list of questions to encourage individual discovery or group participation.
Personal Application Questions—an aid to applying the knowledge gained through study to one's personal living. (Note: These are important questions for group members to answer for themselves, even if they do not wish to discuss their responses in the meeting.)
Focus on Prayer—suggestions for turning one's learning into prayer.

Assignment—activities or preparation to complete prior to the next session.

Here are a few tips which can help you more effectively lead small group studies:

Pray for each group member, asking the Lord to help you create an open atmosphere where everyone will feel free to share with one another and you.

Encourage group members to bring their Bibles as well as their texts to each session. This study is based on the *New International Version*, but it is good to have several translations on hand for purposes of comparison.

Start and end on time. This is especially important for the first meeting because it will set the pattern for the rest of the sessions.

Begin with prayer, asking the Holy Spirit to open hearts and minds and to give understanding so that truth will be applied.

Involve everyone. As learners, we retain only 10% of what we hear; 20% of what we see; 65% of what we hear and see; but 90% of what we hear, see, and do.

Promote a relaxed environment. Arrange the chairs in a circle or semicircle. This allows eye contact among members and encourages dynamic discussion. Be relaxed in your own attitude and manner. Be willing to share yourself.

C   H   A   P   T   E   R   1

A Collective Work

Chapter Theme:

Scripture affirms it is impossible for a Christian to lose his or her salvation because of the sovereign decree of the Father, the ongoing intercession by the Son, and the seal of the Spirit.

Icebreakers

1. Imagine you are engaged to be married in a few months. Although your fiancée knows you to be a man of integrity, she frequently expresses her doubts that you will live up to the promise that the ring on her finger represents. How would you feel?

2. A little boy is working hard to compete in the spelling bee at school. Spelling doesn't come easily to him, and sometimes he refuses to discipline himself to do better. That discourages him to the point of fearing he will never finish school. His father is the principal of the school and is kind, just, and wise. He has repeatedly promised to help his son to do well. The boy, however, refuses to be convinced. What would you say to him?

Group Discovery Questions

1. Should what the Bible teaches regarding divine election restrain anyone from coming to Christ? Why or why not?

2. What is God's will regarding those who believe in Christ? (John 6:40)

3. Respond biblically to the notion that though John 10 says believers rest securely in the Father's hands, it is possible that some could wiggle out.

4. In what way does Jesus anchor the believer to God?

5. To whom does Jesus' prayer of protection in John 17 extend?

6. Explain the significance of a seal in relation to a promise not yet completely fulfilled.

7. What did Augustine say about assurance and why?

Personal Application Questions

1. Do you tend to accept at face value the promises of Scripture regarding eternal security, or are you more apt to think they are too good to be true—or predicated on a series of conditions that are too difficult to keep? Jesus instructed us to be straightforward, saying, "Simply let your 'Yes' be 'Yes,' and your 'No,' 'No' " (Matt. 5:37). We can trust that His Word is just as direct. It says what it means and means what it says.

2. Have you ever before realized that the entire Trinity is at work on your behalf to secure your salvation? Or to be honest, has your eternal security been more to you a matter of self effort? Realize that to question the eternal security of the believer is to question the ability of our Triune God to accomplish what He sets out to do.

Focus on Prayer

Be in awe before God of His ability to save you from sin not only as a one-time act in the past, but also as an ongoing reality in the present and forever.

Assignment

The Scripture passages cited in this chapter are the key texts that affirm the reality of eternal security. Become very familiar with all of them. Underline them in the book or make a flash card for each one, and systematically commit them to your heart and mind.

C   H   A   P   T   E   R   2

Those Troubling Verses

Chapter Theme:

Passages that seem to contradict the doctrine of eternal security, such as those in Galatians 5, Hebrews 6, John 15, and Matthew 12, do no such thing when properly interpreted. Their intent is to warn those who haven't embraced Christ in faith to do so before it is too late.

Icebreakers

1. Suppose you are the president of a club whose purpose is to serve your community. You notice, however, that many of the people who attend the meetings seem more interested in socializing than serving. How do you think the bylaws of the club should address those people?

2. Let's say that in the same club, some of your most diligent members—your best servants—read the bylaws and fear they aren't worthy of being members anymore because of how much they enjoy socializing with the other members. How would you reassure them?

Group Discovery Questions

1. What was the religious background of those Paul wrote to in Galatia? How had some of them fallen away from the concept of grace?

2. In the era of the early church, explain how it could have been easy for many unbelievers to become a part of church life.

3. Summarize Hannah Hurnard's illustration of how a believer can misapply Scriptures that are intended to warn those who do not yet believe.

4. What group of people are given the severest warning in Scripture?

5. Describe the noncommittal attitude of those mentioned in Hebrews 6:4-5. How do we know they weren't Christians?

6. If Hebrews 6, correctly interpreted, meant that salvation could be lost, what teaching would logically proceed from that? What instead does the passage teach?

7. What will saving faith always produce? Support your answer with Scripture. What does that then tell us about the burned branches in John 15?

8. What was the context of Jesus' discourse about the unpardonable sin? How does that relate to the primary application of the passage? What is the secondary application?

9. Why can't a person who rejects the convicting work of the Spirit become a Christian?

10. What happens when the lights go out in a spiritual sense?

Personal Application Questions

1. Have some of the passages discussed in this chapter troubled you? How do you view them now? Reflect on the fresh insights you have gained on them after reading the chapter, and reread the sections that cover those verses to reinforce what you have learned.

2. How have you gone about interpreting a difficult passage of Scripture? Many people merely read the Bible and don't bother to study what isn't readily apparent from a surface reading. As a way to avoid being one of them, look up "interpretation of the Bible" or "hermeneutics" (the science of interpretation) in an evangelical theological dictionary or Bible encyclopedia. Be sure you know what to do the next time you come across a Scripture passage that troubles you.

Focus on Prayer

Pray for the Lord to give you the drive and ability to be a better interpreter of Holy Scripture. Look for opportunities to develop and practice your skills in "handling accurately the word of truth" (2 Tim. 2:15). Ask the Lord to help you to see that not just as the task of a minister, but as the privilege of every true believer.

Assignment

Make a photocopy of the article or articles you read on correctly interpreting the Bible. Keep them next to your Bible as a guide in studying more in depth one of the passages described in this chapter. Before beginning your study, have at hand whatever reference books the article recommends.

C   H   A   P   T   E   R   3

The Ties That Bind

Chapter Theme:
Romans 5:1-11 gives six indicators that show God finishes what He starts in salvation.

Icebreakers
1. You are an engineer trying to win a contract to erect a building. You have successfully constructed many buildings like it, several of which are far more elaborate than the one you are bidding for. The customer, however, is unsure of your ability to get the job done. How would you convince him?
2. A doctor recently saved her patient from certain death. Although the patient's legs are now paralyzed, the doctor is sure that the patient will walk again. The patient is grateful to the doctor for saving his life, but refuses to believe the doctor's reassuring words about being able to walk. You as a nurse have been observing their conversation. How might you reason with the patient so he will believe what the doctor says?

Group Discovery Questions
1. What is the context of Paul's discussion of eternal security in Romans 5:1-11?
2. Explain how continued faith and the Lord's faithfulness work together.
3. What are the objective and subjective aspects of peace with God?
4. Why was the concept of direct access to God so phenomenal to Paul's Jewish readers? Into what state is the believer ushered before God? (Rom. 5:2)
5. What is the end result of salvation? What will happen in the believer's life until that hope is realized? (Rom. 5:2-5)
6. What does the fact of God's love before salvation imply about His love after salvation? (Rom. 5:5-8)

7. Explain Paul's reasoning from the greater to the lesser in
Romans 5:9-10. How does that relate to assurance?
8. What emotion is appropriate in response to being forever
reconciled to God? (Rom. 5:11)

Personal Application Questions
1. Have you ever thought that you could lose your salvation?
Why? Read Romans 5:1-11 and review this chapter, noting how
they address whatever has shaken your assurance in the past.
2. Do you have a tendency to be inconsistent in believing God
for the greater things (such as salvation), but not for the lesser
(such as food, clothing, and shelter)? Note how Jesus reasoned
through similar issues in His Sermon on the Mount (Matt. 6:25-
34).

Focus on Prayer
Ask God to help you be biblically and logically consistent in
what you think and say. Don't allow yourself to believe, for
example, that God is great enough to save you, but not great
enough to keep you saved.

Assignment
To help you establish a biblical mind-set on eternal security,
make a chart with headings that reflect the truths of Romans
5:1-11: the believer's peace with God, standing in grace, hope of
glory, possession of divine love, certainty of deliverance, and joy
in God. Under those headings, write down what Scripture says
elsewhere on those topics. Indicate whatever comes to mind at
first, and then consult a concordance to round out your chart.
Keep it handy in your Bible and use it to confront any fears that
arise over your eternal state.

C H A P T E R   4

The Inevitable Glory

Chapter Theme:
Romans 8:28-30 declares that our salvation is so secure, we can speak of our future glorification as if it has already happened.

Icebreaker
You are about to marry into a family that once was at odds with your family. Although the wedding is still a couple of months away, your future father and mother-in-law have already started referring to you as their son or daughter. How does that make you feel?

Group Discovery Questions
1. What does it mean that God is sovereign?
2. What does our security depend on? (Heb. 6:17-18)
3. What do many people think salvation is predicated on? Respond to that belief biblically.
4. In what ways will we be conformed to Christ? What is the significance of the word "image" in Romans 8:29?
5. What do some people suggest about God's foreknowledge? What problems are we left with?
6. Where does the faith God foresees come from?
7. How does foreknowledge relate to God's love for us?
8. How does God's call from eternity come to us in time?
9. What does it mean to be justified?
10. How can Romans 8:30 describe all believers as already glorified?

Personal Application Questions
1. Romans 8:30 says that those whom God justified He also glorified. We can definitely trust God for our eternal security. Do you have the same kind of trust in God for the temporal things of day-to-day life? In what ways do you show a lack of

confidence in God? Do you, for instance, tend to worry? What are you telling God when you don't trust Him fully? Cultivate a habit of trusting God in every aspect of your life. Since He can guarantee your future glorification, He certainly can take care of you in your present circumstances.

2. One of God's purposes in salvation is to create an eternally redeemed humanity that will glorify Christ forever. Why is Christ worthy of such an honor? How often do you focus on glorifying Him?

Focus on Prayer

Make a list of things you can praise Christ for, and then lift them up to Him in prayer. Thank Him especially that your salvation is as good as done, and ask Him to help you live like you believe that by experiencing assurance on an ongoing basis.

Assignment

Pick up where the chapter leaves off by studying—not just reading—Romans 8:31-39. Note especially the logic of verses 31-34 and the triumphant tone of verses 35-39 as biblical bases for assurance.

C H A P T E R   5

Eleven Tests from an Apostolic Expert

Chapter Theme:

The Book of 1 John presents a series of practical tests to determine the presence of saving faith. Passing those tests is the gateway to assurance.

Icebreakers

1. Suppose a skilled government employee, who had passed many tests and government ratings, began fearing she wasn't worthy of her pension. You are her supervisor. How would you seek to allay her fears?

2. You are a teacher who has assigned a failing grade to one of your students because he failed the tests and quizzes you gave to the class. The student is outraged. He figured that because he was attending a school with a very good academic reputation, he was bound to succeed. He is now in your office confronting you. What would you say to him?

Group Discovery Questions

1. What did Jonathan Edwards say is the supreme proof of true conversion? How does that relate to assurance?

2. What are some of the signs of experiencing fellowship with God and Christ?

3. How does the believer regard sin in his or her life?

4. How does obedience relate to assurance? What is the believer's primary motivation for obedience?

5. How will a true Christian feel toward the world system and why?

6. Explain the believer's heavenward perspective and how that relates to life here on earth.

7. Explain the difference between sinning frequently and prac-

ticing sin. What is the implication regarding assurance?

8. What virtue in your life will soothe a condemning heart? (1 John 3:17-21)

9. How can answered prayer bring assurance?

10. How does the Holy Spirit minister to the believer?

11. How does a true believer regard everything he or she sees, hears, and reads? Why?

12. What does suffering for what is right indicate?

Personal Application Question

Have you tended to base your salvation on a past event rather than the present course of your life? If so, rethink how to explain your testimony in a biblical way so that you're prepared the next time someone asks you how you became a Christian.

Focus on Prayer

Ask the Lord to help you objectively evaluate your Christian life in light of the tests in 1 John.

Assignment

Even if you're sure of the outcome, take all eleven tests presented in this chapter. Doing so is a healthy, biblical exercise (2 Cor. 13:5). Write down your answers here in summary form. Use them to encourage yourself should you ever struggle with doubts about your salvation. However, if you've failed any of the tests, take the matter very seriously. Deal immediately and decisively with whatever you've uncovered (cf. 2 Cor. 6:2).

C H A P T E R 6

Dealing with Doubt

Chapter Theme:
When struggling with the insecure feeling of not knowing for sure if you will go to heaven, it helps to know the different reasons that could lead you to question your salvation.

Icebreaker
Think back to your elementary school days, and picture yourself talking with a friend who doubts that his parents love him anymore. You have met his parents several times when playing with your friend at his home, and know them to be a very loving family. What could you encourage your friend to focus on in his life to help him understand why he's feeling the way he is?

Group Discovery Questions
1. In what way can strong preaching unsettle the assurance of some who hear it? Discuss the pros and cons of that.
2. How does Satan use guilt to promote doubt?
3. Why does ignorance of the sovereignty of God in salvation undermine assurance?
4. How does the resurrection of Christ play a role in assurance?
5. Should your assurance depend heavily on recalling the exact moment of your salvation? Explain your answer.
6. How can Romans 7 be understood in an imbalanced way? How can you maintain a balance regarding the flesh's influence?
7. In what sense do trials actually strengthen assurance rather than undermine it?
8. How is it possible to short-circuit the Holy Spirit's ministry of assurance?
9. What is assurance the reward for?
10. Fill in the blanks: High degrees of _____ cannot be enjoyed by those who persist in low levels of _____.
11. What is an especially practical way of dealing with sin?

Personal Application Questions

1. Recall the last time you felt insecure about your eternal state. Was that feeling associated with strong but imbalanced preaching, guilt, ignorance of the divine aspect of salvation, uncertainty in not knowing the exact time of your salvation, temptation, certain trials, fleshliness, or disobedience? Isolate whichever of those areas trouble you most, and think about them in light of Scripture to protect you from future bouts with insecurity.

2. Do trials tend to unsettle you emotionally? Are they one of the factors that trouble you most about your assurance? If so, think carefully about whether trials in general upset you or if it's only certain types of trials you're apt to respond to with feelings of insecurity. Should you discover that you almost always have trouble responding in a godly way toward financial, interpersonal, or other kinds of pressures, recall that "no temptation has overtaken you but such as is common to man; and God is faithful, who will not allow you to be tempted beyond what you are able, but with the temptation will provide the way of escape also, that you may be able to endure it" (1 Cor. 10:13).

Focus on Prayer

Instead of letting yourself be overwhelmed by feelings of doubt over your salvation, ask the Lord to help you think clearly and biblically about what is causing those feelings.

Assignment

To replace your feelings with fact, take yourself through the catechism on assurance that concludes the chapter. Once you have finished reading it out loud, write out just the questions. Answer the questions in your own words, jotting down as many Scriptures as you can think of to support your answers.

C H A P T E R   7

Adding Virtue upon Virtue

Chapter Theme:
To enjoy assurance here and great spiritual reward hereafter, 2 Peter 1 instructs the believer to diligently pursue the virtues that produce a fruitful Christian life.

Icebreakers
1. How would you feel if you provided food, clothing, and shelter to a destitute group of people who at first well received all you offered, but then neglected to use what you gave them?
2. Suppose you have a gifted teenager who was selected for the lead in a school play. While she has a love for the theater, has been well-trained, and is able to deliver an outstanding performance, she decides to forsake the part and do the bare minimum to get a passing grade in her theater class. What would you say to motivate her to reconsider her decision?

Group Discovery Questions
1. Why is remembrance such a vital aspect of Christian ministry?
2. How does the command in 2 Peter 1:5 to apply all diligence correspond with all that God has already done for us, as described in verses 3-4?
3. Why is excellence more an action than an attitude?
4. What is the danger of living by emotions rather than by knowledge and right thinking?
5. What are some practical tips for developing self-control? Explain each.
6. Explain the idea behind the Greek word translated "perseverance" in 2 Peter 1:6.
7. How does godliness relate to worship?
8. Explain the connection between love and friendship, then

apply that to the concept of discipleship.

9. What is most indicative of true salvation? (2 Peter 1:8; Matt. 7:15-20)

10. Explain the phenomenon of spiritual amnesia and the antidote to it (2 Peter 1:9-10).

11. How does present obedience relate to future spiritual reward?

Personal Application Questions

1. Do you have the tendency to just slide by in most aspects of your life, or are you more apt to pursue excellence? After thinking carefully about that, look to the example of the Apostle Paul, who wrote, "One thing I do: Forgetting what is behind and straining toward what is ahead, I press on toward the goal to win the prize for which God has called me heavenward in Christ Jesus. All of us who are mature should take such a view of things" (Phil. 3:13-15, NIV).

2. What kind of fruit are you bearing in your Christian life? Focus on what God considers true spiritual fruit as revealed in 2 Peter 1: diligence, excellence, knowledge, self-control, perseverance, godliness, and love.

Focus on Prayer

Ask the Lord to help you make the most of your short life on earth (James 4:14) that at the end He might say to you, "Well done, good and faithful slave" (Matt. 25:21). Don't regard such an acknowledgment as a given, but as something to work toward every day.

Assignment

Compare the virtues listed in 2 Peter 1:5-7 with the fruit of the Spirit listed in Galatians 5:22-23 for a clearer understanding of what God wants to see in your life. Evaluate how you're doing in manifesting each of those spiritual character qualities. You may want to ask a close friend or family member to help you so that you can be more objective. Make a note of the areas you are

weakest in; then pursue each as a theme throughout Scripture—
the goal being to know and then to do the will of God more
perfectly.

C   H   A   P   T   E   R   8

Gaining Victory

Chapter Theme:
Nothing provides greater assurance than seeing results. God's Spirit enables the believer to experience victory in spite of the residual sin in his or her life.

Icebreakers
1. If you were asked to undertake a great task, would you make much headway if you felt like you were set up to lose? What kind of attitude would motivate you to do your best at completing the task?
2. Imagine this: You have lived in a war zone all of your life and been engaged in a losing battle since your earliest memory. Then you enlist the aid of a mighty conqueror who has always been successful in defeating your enemy. How would the conqueror expect you to regard his abilities and his direct instructions to you?

Group Discovery Questions
1. Explain the pattern of bad news then good news in God's revealed truth regarding salvation and sanctification. How does that affect the salvation assurance of some believers?
2. Why is a victim mentality so deadly to personal spiritual growth?
3. In what ways is sin deceitful?
4. Explain the concept of being consistent in dealing with sin.
5. Describe the role of the Word and prayer in poisoning and exposing sin.
6. What transition takes place in moving from a private to a public arena in dealing with the sin in your life?
7. What are some practical questions to ask yourself in discerning how effective you now are in gaining victory over sin?

Personal Application Questions

1. Does it disturb you to realize that the Christian life is not as easy as you perhaps first expected or hoped for? Be comforted in realizing that you had to have effectively handled the bad news of sin if you received the good news of salvation. God's Spirit is present in your life to help you be just as effective in dealing with sin in your life now that you are a believer.

2. Are you more apt to make excuses for the sin in your life or do you tend to be aggressive in dealing with it? If the first, carefully reread and think through the chapter section on avoiding a victim mentality. If the second, reinforce that good habit by reconsidering the section on the deceitfulness of sin. As good as it is to deal effectively with the sins you know that you struggle with, it is a spiritual step up to seek awareness of sins troubling you that you don't yet recognize.

Focus on Prayer

Make David's prayer your own: "Search me, O God, and know my heart; try me, and know my thoughts; and see if there be any wicked way in me" (Ps. 139:23). God is sure to answer that prayer since it is according to His will (cf. 1 John 5:14). As He does, ask Him to help you maintain a balance in being repentant but not excessively sorrowful (cf. 2 Cor. 7:9-10).

Assignment

Take out a sheet of paper and write or type your answers to the personal inventory that closes the chapter. Think carefully about your answers, and don't be afraid to be honest. Use God's Word and prayer to encourage you in the areas where you are strong, and to give direction for change wherever you are weak.

C H A P T E R   9

Persevering through It All

Chapter Theme:
Without a doubt, God enables all true believers to remain faithful to Christ, endure any difficulty, and receive eternal life in the end.

Icebreakers
1. Suppose you are running in a race or some other contest of endurance. What motivates you to persevere when you start to feel uncomfortable or experience pain?
2. Let's say you are a supervisor instructing an employee who is afraid he won't be able to handle the job you are assigning him. You are confident that he can. How would you try to convince him? What attitude would you want him to adopt?

Group Discovery Questions
1. What brings happiness in relation to trials? Why?
2. How is the doctrine of the perseverance of the saints related to eternal security?
3. What does the Old Testament say about God's preserving His people for life? How is that reinforced in the New?
4. How is the perseverance of the saints related to the predestinating work of God? Explain the problems that arise from not maintaining a balance between those two biblical truths.
5. What is the reward for perseverance?

Personal Application Questions
1. If you take God at His Word that He will help you through whatever happens in your life, you won't tend to worry about big or little things. After taking an honest look at your life, would you and those close to you be obliged to characterize you as a worrier? If so, the next time you catch yourself worrying, stop and realize that whatever is troubling you is an opportunity

Saved Without a Doubt

to see God at work in your life. Cultivate that habit as one way of refusing to let worry dominate your life any longer.

2. Think about what has made you feel happy over the past few weeks. Was your response to a trial—and the outcome of that trial—one of the things that came to mind? If not, look at the next trial that comes your way not as something to be feared, but as something that can produce great personal blessing and assurance.

Focus on Prayer

Ask the Lord to bring to mind what you have learned in this chapter whenever you experience fear or anxiety from a new trial in your life. As you meditate on those truths, develop an attitude of confidence in God's ability to enable you to persevere.

Assignment

Carefully reread the ready reference of Scriptures that illustrate God at work on our behalf. Take out your calendar and make a plan for memorizing approximately one Scripture per week until you have memorized them all. When you face difficulty, they will be invaluable in assisting you to replace negative emotions with confidence.

SCRIPTURE INDEX

S U B J E C T   I N D E X

Access, divine, 43–44
Adoption, spiritual, 104–5
Affliction. See Trials
Amnesia, spiritual, 125–26
Arminian theology, 9–10
Assurance of salvation
  blessings of, 129–31
  catechism on, 107–9
  doubts regarding, 7–12, 95–109, 127, 130–31
  experiencing, 9, 95–153
  false, 8–9, 95
  importance of, 8, 100, 127
  objective and subjective grounds for, 11–12, 98
  righteousness and, 10–12, 33, 111–32
  "syllogistic," 9
Augustine, on assurance, 21

Barclay, William
  on diligence 114–15
  on perseverance, 120–21
Barnhouse, Donald Grey, regarding a Zulu chief whose son was
  captured, 41
Bauckham, Richard, on spiritual amnesia, 126
Berkhof, Louis, on perseverance, 149
Berkhouwer, G.C., on Catholicism and assurance, 10
Blasphemy, against the Holy Spirit, 34–37
Bridge, William, on lacking assurance, 96–97
Brooks, Thomas, on lacking assurance, 97–98, 105–6
Bunyan, John, his fear of committing the unpardonable sin,
  34–35

Calling, divine, 60–61
Catholic theology, regarding assurance, 10
Correction, accepting, 119